"Angie's Miniature Challenges"
Magazine Projects

Part 2: 2001-2005 and beyond

Dedication.

To Hazel and John Dowd and all the Minis4All 'gang'. XXXs

Publishing Data

First published 2016 Sliding Scale Books (SSPB05)

Plaza De Andalucia 1, Campofrio, 21668, Huelva, Spain.

(c) Copyright Angie Scarr 2000-2016
Text and step-by-step photography Angie Scarr 2000-2016
Additional photography Frank Fisher
Design by Frank Fisher and Angie Scarr

Sliding Scale SSPB05

Contents

"Angie's Miniature Challenges"
Magazine Projects 2000-2005 & beyond

Foreword to part 2
by Betsy Niederer

When Angie asked me to write this introduction for her new book I was honored and thrilled to say yes! She taught me just about everything I know about making miniature food. Above all else she showed me that with practice I could make pretty much whatever I wanted out of polymer clay.

You can learn to make miniature dollhouse food no matter what your skill level. Angie's instructions are simple and straightforward and with practice you will end up with results that you never thought possible. The key to success is practice. One of the things that I love about Angie is her philosophy that you can do it, because you really can!

Angie has been one of the pioneers in this art, demonstrated by her innovative techniques and generous teaching skills. Most of the highly skilled miniature food artists working right now are using techniques that were first developed by Angie, and we all owe her our thanks.

Introduction to part 2 of Miniature Challenges
by Angie Scarr.

When I was editing the challenges series for book I it was strange to have to edit out words and expressions which are already a little archaic, expressions about the internet and surfing! It became clear that often I am presenting these ideas to a whole new generation of miniaturists. But as we go through the series the ideas evolved as did my style of presentation. More often in this second half the ideas were set out as step by step projects after the publication of my first book Making Miniature Food and Market Stalls.

Part 2 takes up where we left off with challenges and other magazine articles from December 2001 onwards.

The larger part of this collection is taken from the "Challenge Angie" series of articles originally published in the "Dolls House And Miniature Scene" magazine, but I've also included articles originally published in other miniatures magazines both British and American and have mentioned the magazine in every case and issue number where I've been able to work that out, although many or all of these issues are sold out. For the print version of this

book we added 3 projects from 2012 that had not been printed before outside of magazines. They were part of a fresh series of challenges, the remainder are already in my Colour Book.

We took my original version of the text before any editing by magazine editors as our start, and altered that as little as possible to keep the 'blogging' style that I had then.

Not every project gives the step-by-step instructions. In some cases a note about the way I now do things now has been added, where it makes a significant improvement on the results. Many however are just a taste of the methods which are explored more thoroughly in my books.

Where there is an important link to the books or to YouTube videos I have added these links to the text.

I hope you enjoy this look back at past challenges. I'm looking forward to writing more books in this format and to being able to present translations into other languages in the near future.

Please feel free to contact me with any comments or requests for information via my webform or on facebook

www.angiescarr.co.uk

facebook.com/angiescarr.miniatures

www.youtube.com/user/angiescarr

Best wishes, Angie.

"Angie's Miniature Challenges"
Magazine Projects

Part 2: 2001-2005 & beyond

Kiwi Fruit

Originally published in DHMS Magazine Issue 90 December 2001

Kiwi fruits did not originate in New Zealand

Apparently Kiwi fruits were a native of China and were improved by the New Zealanders. Kiwis are small oval fruits with a thin brown hairy skin, soft green flesh and purplish-black seeds. Not the best challenge for me because I'm actually allergic to them. I've a feeling it's just to their hairiness. You'll have to ask my hirsute husband, Frank, if I overreact to him too!

I don't remember seeing Kiwi fruits in England until the seventies, and it is only very recently that they have become common in our local shops. Although supermarkets have stocked them regularly for about a decade, certainly you would not find them in a period doll's house. So this project is really for those with a passion for 'caning' in Polymer clay.

According to my e-friend Jane in Perth, Australia, kiwi fruits are eaten like boiled eggs over there. You cut the top off and scoop the flesh out with a special spoon.

On my website angiescarr.co.uk there are also YouTube videos of making kiwis.

Step 1

If you look carefully at a kiwi (you should see me at the dinner table examining all my food) you will see that it is made up of many sections each with a tiny seed in. In fact there are several seeds in each section but you only need to make one small cylinder of purple or black. For the flesh, I mixed a very pale green from a scrap each of leaf green and yellow with lots of translucent Fimo. I carefully pressed this into a v shaped strip

which I cut in half and surrounded the 'seed' part with these two pieces.

Step 2

You can see that I used a paintbrush to make a hollow in each half at the narrow edge. This keeps the cylinder shape for the seed.

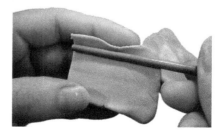

Step 3

I then added a strip of white to one side. This is to divide the segments. This whole strip needs lengthening by a combination of squeezing, smoothing and pulling (I'm afraid you can't roll this one!).

Step 4

When you have enough length to cut it into about twelve sections (so that's at least twelve inches long)

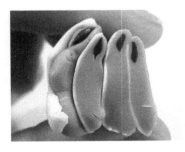

Step 5

cut and stack the sections together to form a near crescent shape, or half a hollow cylinder. Try not to get any air trapped between these sections.

You'll need to press this and lengthen this again and cut it in half. Alternatively, you could make up the whole cylinder in one.

Step 6

For the centre you need a small cylinder of a more opaque, paler green. I recommend a mix of translucent with a small amount of white and a tiny amount of the green mix you used for the flesh. Be careful not to make this central cylinder too big which I did first time round.

Wrap the central cylinder with the prepared outer parts and then add the skin. What a shame that Fimo discontinued their caramel colour as this is the perfect outer skin for the Kiwi. You can mix a reasonably reliable substitute using two parts terracotta (now called chocolate), one part ochre and a small piece of leaf green.

Step 7

Regular readers of this column or my book will be away on their own by now! The cylinder is lengthened by squeezing the centre of the cylinder quite firmly and then working outwards. Don't roll the cylinder

until you have squeezed it fairly firmly all the way along otherwise all your carefully prepared sections will move against each other and cause a jumble.

Step 8

Make the tiny fruit by enclosing the end of the cylinder and then cutting a piece off and closing the other end. Don't forget that a kiwi fruit is not quite round but rather flattened.

Step 9

A hairy appearance can be added using brown scenic scatter as in the picture. I do something which I probably shouldn't recommend, so I'm not going to, in case you all decide to die of some horrible Fimo dust induced lung disease or something. So,

just for your interest I grind a dust from lightly cooked caramel colour Fimo to roll my Kiwi fruit in.

Step 10

Finally I noticed the ends have a tiny 'wiggly' dark brown flower part so I added that just before cutting my Kiwi in half.

Step 11

If you leave off the skin you can make a long cane which you can cut into fruit slices, (for tarts etc.) along with last month's strawberries [see book part I of this series].

Xmas

*Originally published in DHMS Magazine
Issue 91 January 2002*

Christmas comes early for the miniaturist.

I have to admit it, I'm ignoring for the moment the many exciting and interesting challenges that are still awaiting my attention. From Big Macs to Stargazy pie. Lettuce to Laurel wreaths. Challenges which I'd love to have a go at but which I'll have to leave for that delightful time between 'Ally Pally' and February. Actually, that should be just about now, by the time you read this. You can imagine me wallowing in a roomful of polymer clay daydreaming and producing more mad miniatures. "Here Angie, just spin this into gold would you" ... There I go, living in my fantasy world! So rushed, as usual, I'm cheating a bit and just showing you what I'm doing right now, and hope you'll forgive me until the new year.

Christmas comes early for the miniaturist and for the miniaturist's magazines as well as for the shops. So, although It's only October as I write this, I'm already late for Christmas! By the way, If any one is offering to buy you polymer clay for Christmas make sure they know that translucent is the most important colour!

Step 1

If you're lucky enough to receive some you'd better go and raid the cupboards for some poppy seeds, or any other tiny seeds will do. If you have some tiny red glass beads they look good as cherries. You can use either the seed beads you can get at haberdashers which look rather like cut cherries when embedded into the clay, or the really tiny red beads I've used here are from Tee Pee crafts. You need at least brown clay.

You can chop this up finely with a little black and a little cream coloured clay. I must admit I get a little frustrated when I'm asked for colour mixes for things like cakes which have many different shades. My suggestion is you cut yourself a large slice and look at it for a short time ... before stuffing it into your already overfed self and washing down with a cup of tea (at least that's what I do)!

I'm also asked every month for the names of suppliers of the bits and bobs I use so I'll mention as many as I can this month in the hope that I get Christmas cards from them (bottles of whiskey ... chocolates ... mmmm)!

Step 2

And as for quantities, the question is, do you want to make one cake, or ten? If you're a beginner, conserving your meagre clay supplies I suggest you start small. Remember that the inside of the cake is going to be maybe around 2 centimetres square by one deep, so you won't need a lot. You need to recombine your chopped mixture and then chop again rather a lot

of times until, from a distance, you can't tell that there is more than one colour. Roll the mixture out until it is around a centimetre deep and then cut out your square (or rectangle or circle).

Step 3

The Marzipan is, in this case, a basic mix of translucent with a little white and a tiny bit of ochre.

Step 4

You need to roll this and cut it out just as you would for a real cake.

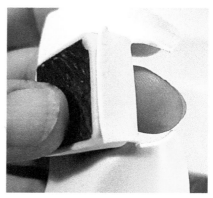

Step 5

When you have put the marzipan on and kept the cake a nice sharp square. Now you really do need to wash your hands and make sure you're not wearing anything with fibres that 'shed'. Believe me, every tiny speck of dust will find it's way to your work as if to spite you!

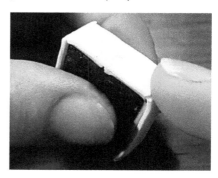

Step 6

You can shortcut the icing (white and translucent) by making a larger square and putting the cake on it upside down. Then you can cut out the corner squares and turn the cake back the right way up. Then your nice clean fingers can be used to smooth the edges together.

Now you have a nice blank cake which you can decorate any way you like. Here I've used painted brass holly leaves from

last 's').

There were two sizes of little fluffy balls and I mounted them on an earring shaft. I tied thread round his neck and put some more of those tiny black beads on for eyes and buttons. I must admit that I ran out of patience just before the carrot!

You can pick up and place the beads with the licked end of a piece of uncooked spaghetti. These beads seem to have no end of uses!

Petite Fleur. The poinsettia I made from two, four-petalled flower shapes which I cut out from some of that sticky backed flock material but you could use paper and craft glue just as effectively. Some more of the very tiny beads, this time in gold, made the centre. The ribbon was bought from a local shop.

Step 7

The organdie ribbon on the tiny round cake was from a miniature fair. (I think, but then my drawers are full of things I 'just picked up'.)

Step 9

The walnut bowl is actually coriander seeds. I selected and glued the largest with PVA glue, and one of Andrew Gregory's beautiful, working nutcrackers!
[Sadly Andrew is no longer with us but his beautiful cast items sit in many collections and are a testament to his perfectionism]

Step 8

The little Snowman was made from three purchases made on the same day from a local favourite shop which seems to sell just about everything, known locally as Boyses. (That's Hessle Road speak for 'Boyes' the sign for which remains confusingly un-punctuated but which I suspect should have it's apostrophe just before the

Simnel Cake

Originally published in DHMS Magazine Issue 94 April 2002

Here's a really simple simnel cake just as my mother used to make full size. I used to love the lightly toasted marzipan. By the way, did you know you can make edible marzipan baskets in a bun tray and bake them lightly and fill them with minia-ture marzipan fruits that you can eat? Yum! I made some as a Christmas gift one year but they would be equally appropriate for Easter.

Here's a really simple simnel cake.

I have had several requests for more polymer clay cakes and buns. I think this is because many of you have 'tea shoppes'. I have to admit bakery is not my strong suit either in life or in 'twelfth'. There really are hundreds of miniaturists who do it way better than me.

However there are two real reasons for putting in a cake this month. One is because it's Easter time (yes I know this mag is dated April but we all know you get it well before Easter don't we?) and the other is to lure Jan, our new editor, into a false sense of security. You see Jan is a very nice lady and I'm not sure she knows what she's letting herself in for. She's not quite aware of just how screwy us miniaturists can be.

I was explaining that the most popular challenges were not the pretty fruits and 'cakies' but the slimy looking squid and the dead-eyed boars head. Her nose wrinkled very slightly. So Jan, here's my first chal-lenge for you, before I hit you with the full eccentricity of your esteemed readership! (Back to normal next month).

Step 1

You will need a light mix of champagne and ochre clays plus translucent with a good pinch of poppy seeds well mixed in for each cake. Roll the mixture out until it is just a little more than a quarter of an inch thick (around 7mm). You'll need a circular cutter, or you could make a square simnel cake just by cutting out squares of about three quarters of an inch (or 2cm) these sizes aren't critical just remember you rarely get a cake in real life that's as big as twelve inches across so you need to

keep well within an inch in twelfth scale.

When cutting out use talcum powder on your cutters to help release the clay. Then roll out a thin sheet of 'marzipan' made from a mix of 75% translucent and 25% white with just a little ochre added.

Step 2

As you can see the edges are merely twists made from rolled out mixture.

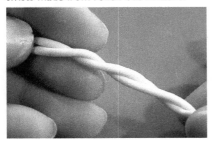

Step 3

This bit requires a little practise and you should make a long strip and use the best bit!

Cook the cake. That is to say oven-set it according to the instructions on your clay packet. (You can wait until you have made the chick and the egg and set them all together though not assembled.).

When the cake is cooked you can add

the glaze very subtly to the marzipan. I use Humbrol clear colour 1322. [Humbrol Clear Colour may not be available now, so just use ochre and brown colour pastels or powder before baking and varnish after]. Make sure there isn't too much glaze on your brush by wiping some off on a tissue before brushing lightly onto the cake and especially it's raised edges.

Step 4

Then down to the tiny chick and his egg. When you think you've made a small enough chick you probably need to make

one half that size! Just two tiny balls of yellow clay. Put a really tiny cone shaped beak on to the smaller ball before you add it to the bigger one. and cook the chick. Or you can cheat and buy some of those tiny pom-poms in yellow from a craft shop and glue on a folded diamond of orange paper.

Step 5

The egg is 50/50 white and translucent. I made a tiny ball of the mixture and used a ball ended tool to hollow it out. You'll need one or even two of these.

Step 6

You snip the edges of the egg after it is cooked to form a jagged 'broken' edge. Make sure you keep the bits.

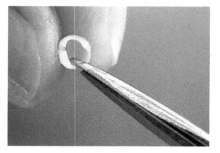

Step 7

Glue the cracked egg and it's 'bits' and the little chick to the top of the cake.

Step 8

The History of the simnel cake.

I had assumed that simnel cake was an Easter tradition but it actually dates back as far as the seventeenth century and was given as a mother's day present on the fourth Sunday in Lent. However since Lent is a time of fasting it seems the cake had to keep until Easter. Although the topping was traditionally an almond marzipan known as 'marchpane'. This presumably was the choice of the rich. Sometimes the crust was simply made of flour and water paste coloured with saffron.

Forced Rhubarb

Originally published in DHMS Magazine Issue 95 May 2002

What Josie wanted was a tiny clump of bright pink forced rhubarb to put under a chimney pot in her doll's house garden. so I dug up a bit and put it on my workbench. The first thing that I noticed was that the sheaths surrounding the new buds were very brown and papery. the whole clump was surrounded by the previous year's die back leaving a mass of dark brown 'shreds'.

Just a little late for season.

Often my challenges appear just a little late for season. My Christmas cake appeared in the January edition and my Easter cake in Aprils issue. By the time you read this we'll be well on our way to summer. However, as I write, the first flowers of spring are just forcing their way through the ground and it looks like spring rain! This time of year sees me trying to save the lives of plants I'd already abandoned (due to overwork) to frosts.

Because I'm always banging on about working from life I had to save Josie Senior's challenge until I could scrabble around under the matting of old straw I'd taken from the rabbit cage and dumped on my own rhubarb plant and find what I needed for the task. The first fat buds of new early rhubarb. 'Ideal for forcing' it said on the label. I had a great crop last year and let me tell you it took no persuasion at all!

Step 1

To simulate this I passed some terracotta (now called chocolate) and a pre mixed lighter brown mix through my pasta maker on the thinnest setting. The pasta maker smoothes softened clay but if the clay is old or cold from the packet

it shreds a little as it passes through first time. I used this effect to simulate the old foliage around the base of the new buds.

Incidentally the lighter brown mix is a colour I use is approximately the same colour as the old Caramel now discontinued by Fimo. The mix for this colour is one

I'm asked for regularly. Fimo themselves recommend a mix of :-

2 parts 77 terracotta (now called chocolate), one part 17 Ochre and about a third of a part 57 Leaf green. The shreds are further chopped up with a blade or the side of a dental tool and piled into a little mound. I used some Mix Quick underneath to 'glue' the bits together and to form a soft base to stick the stalks into. You could use translucent instead of the Mix Quick.

Step 2

The Rhubarb stalks and the buds are quite a bright pink and so although I used the same method as I use to make normal garden rhubarb, making a stripy skinned square cane. I used a much brighter pinkish

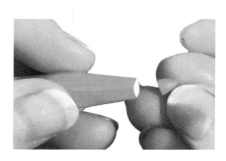

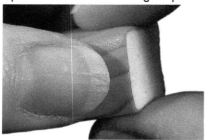

red rather than a dark red for the skin. As I explain in my book Making Miniature Food the stripes are not completely necessary and are barely noticeable so you can get away with making the rhubarb without.

Step 3

When you have lengthened it (very carefully) by smoothing alternate faces of the four sided cane leave it a little short of the required thinness for the main rhubarb stalks and close the skin over the end to form little cones. These cones will form the 'buds' of rhubarb which are just emerg-ing. Do not oven set these in advance). When you have made as many of these as you feel you will need (usually only one or two per plant) ...

Step 4

you can make the stalks by thinning down even more. Don't ask me how thin to make them, just keep going until they snap!

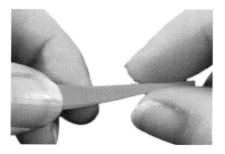

Step 5

Cut out tiny circles of the thinnest possible translucent green. You can make this colour by adding only a tiny bit of green and yellow to a much larger quantity of translucent. You can either roll out the clay as thinly as you can and cut with a

small circle cutter or you can make a log of the green and cut the material as a thin slice from the log. The size does not have to be exact because you will be crumpling the leaf anyway. If you have a leaf veiner (there are several styles available on my website angiescarr.co.uk and some YouTube examples of using them too) you can vein and then crumple the leaf.

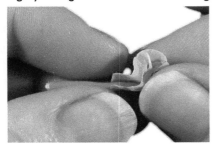

Step 6

If you don't have a veiner, you can attach the leaf to the end of the stalk and then simply crumple the leaf over the end slightly curling the end as if the whole thing

is just unfolding. These stalks should be oven set before adding to the mound.

Step 7

The buds you made earlier should be stuck on to the top of the mound and extremely thin shavings of the caramel colour should be put around it as if it is just breaking out of its coating. These should be shaved off your colour mix with a single sided blade. Then you can put two or three emerging stalks of different lengths surrounding the bud. It's a good idea to put a little more of the very fine caramel shavings around the base of the stalks.

If you want to make standard (non-forced) rhubarb in it's growing state you can follow the same method but make the stalks a deeper red and the leaves a darker green with a more open leaf. You will need to use a veiner for these leaves.

A note on the history of rhubarb which seems so very happy and at home in Britain particularly in Wakefield, West Yorkshire which produced over 50,000 tons annually at one time. Rhubarb as a plant was first introduced into Britain from Russia and China as early as the 16th century and the plants were grown medicinally to produce a cure for many ills including constipation and VD. It seems however, as a culinary 'fruit' (though strictly a vegetable) it didn't become popular until Victorian times when it was discovered that blanching the stems by depriving them of light produced a more tender and colourful crop. So unless you're making a miniature physician's garden it is probably best to avoid the rhubarb in any dollshouse scene set before 1800.

Crown Roast Of Lamb

Originally published in DHMS Magazine Issue 96 June 2002

I'm rather hoping that Hugh Fearnley-Whittingstall will invite me to some big cook-in at River Cottage ...

Although I have been asked for Crown Roast of lamb several times I never quite got round to it. How could I resist Jude White's recent request though. Jude has written to me several times and her letters are always peppered with little smiley faces. Jude also recently sent me a nice little stamp she had made from an imprint of the top of a button. This one had a thistle motif. Jude came up with the idea of stamping an impression on tiny circles of Fimo to produce Shortbreads. I think it will also make nice, old fashioned butter 'pats'. Many thanks Jude, and I hope you don't mind me passing on this idea. So, we'll all be raiding the family button box this week. If you come up with any similar ideas why not let me know and I'll pass them on.

I've never had Crown Roast myself as it is a large dinner party presentation. And I've never given, nor been asked to a large dinner party! I'm rather hoping that Hugh Fearnley-Whittingstall will invite me to some big cook-in at River cottage when he kills the fatted sheep. Until then I had to content myself with a thorough search of the Internet where I found a Welsh Butcher who had wonderfully detailed illustrations of the real thing 'in the raw', as well as many other cuts of meat (great source of information for my butchery items) I do have a problem as a British miniaturist though, as some of our 'cuts' are not the same as those in the many parts of the world that this publication, and my miniatures, reach!

I understood the principle of the thing, but couldn't remember whether the meat part of the chop was on the outside or the inside. Well, in case you're wondering too. it's on the inside. That is to say that the rack of chops is twisted around into the crown shape and tied with string with the bones on the outside and meat part innermost. Usually the crown is made up of two racks. Altogether 16-18 chops and would weigh between 3-5lbs in total. So, these days an expensive dish!

Step 1

This was not a terribly difficult challenge for me as I already make lamb chops as a cane and so simply needed to ensure

that the bones were the right shape. I decided to make my chops by my usual method of laying down the various layers...

Step 2

Make the bones by cutting a piece of creamy quite translucent clay to the right thickness and cut strips from it.

Step 3

Make a triangle of meat coloured clay and stick the bones to it.

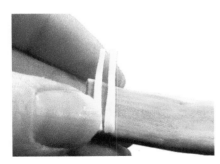

Step 4

Wrap the bones in a thin layer of trans-lucent + ochre skin.

Step 5

Form the whole around into a crown.

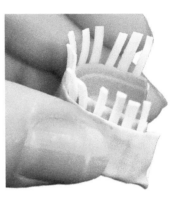

Step 6

The little paper 'chef's hats' as I call them were also easy to produce with tissue paper. Basically you just cut tiny squares of tissue paper. fold them in half and snip lines to half way across.

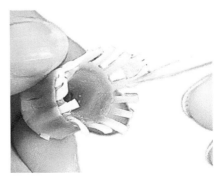

Step 7

I made the rosemary sprigs from tissue paper too. I folded and glued some tissue over a small piece of sugarcraft wire. I painted one side green and left the other side white.

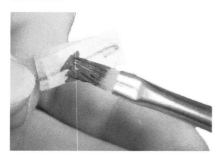

Step 8

When this was dry I cut it into a narrow leaf shape ...

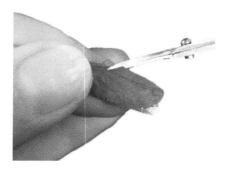

Step 9

and snipped as finely as I could into it all the way up both sides. I simply twisted this a few times with a pair of small pliers.

The roast potatoes were made with the same cream coloured mix. I formed small whole potato shapes which I then cooked. I cut them up while they were still warm from the oven. You should take great care if you do this as you have to use a sharp blade. If you are at all unsteady I suggest you use tweezers or miniature

pliers to hold the pieces as you cut them. I then put the pieces in a small plastic bag with a little watered down craft paint. Since it is rather a long time since I made the potatoes I decided to check whether the 'Citadel' colour I used was the one

called 'Flesh Wash' or 'Snakebite Leather'. I'm still uncertain which I used but I did discover why flesh wash is so called having thoroughly covered myself in the stuff as I tried to replace the cap! I was lucky enough to be given a large box of half used miniature gaming colours which were so beloved of teenagers during the late eighties/early nineties.(Thanks to my nephew Damien) . The colours include wonderful 'fake blood' colours and all sorts of stuff useful to a miniaturist concentrating on food and for ageing/'grungeing' your miniatures. There are still a few games workshop shops around and these are a very useful source of paints and scenic materials.

Perhaps, kind readers, you will let us know how far back the serving if crown roasts goes in history. I rather suspect that it's a long way since the Tudors were very fond of dressing up their dishes. Who invented the paper frills? This looks like a question for Aileen Tucker! (Merry Gourmet Miniatures)

There is another presentation of these racks of lamb chops called 'Guard of Honour' which is formed with the bones of the two racks of chops interlaced.

Haggis

Originally published in DHMS Magazine Issue 104 February 2003

Here is a great seasonal project.

This was a challenge thrown down at me nearly two years ago by Alan Hannah. (A Scotsman) I thought it was a great idea but then missed the window of opportunity last year.

Isn't it great when a country within a country has a separate culture and so many of its own traditions. I feel almost qualified, although a 'Sassenach' myself to talk about the Haggis. My dad, though very much an Englishman, was regularly invited to our local Burns Club supper on Burns night. This was because my dad was a bit of an entertainer wrote many a slightly risqué monologue which were very popular at the 'Marfleet Burns Club'(In Hull, England). For the benefit of our overseas readers Burns night has almost superseded Hogmanay (New Year's Eve) as the most important celebration of the Scot's calendar. Up there in 'Bonnie Scotland' and all over the world the Scots celebrate their culture and show

their reverence for their favourite poet by toasting him, no doubt in a glass of their own malt whisky, and cooking that most Scottish of dishes The Haggis, served up with mashed 'neaps' (turnips) and 'tatties' (potatoes). Now I know that many of you are going to feel a little queasy at this description of Haggis but believe me it's absolutely delicious.

Haggis is a mixture of sheep's liver and other offal with crushed barley grains and spices all stuffed into part of a sheep's stomach which is then tied off at both ends. The whole thing is then boiled for several hours. It is very tasty and has a nutty texture due to the barley grains. When it's cut open the contents spill out spicy and steaming! Yes I bought one, yes, I cooked it. And of course yes, I tasted it before I started making it! Just in the interests of research you understand.

Featured basket by Zara Ribaud-Thompson

Step 1

A simplified version of my colour mix, which is probably just as effective at 12th scale would be to use a simple brown Fimo with no additional colours. To this I added

as much coarse ground maize as I could get into the mix. Ground maize is available at Delicatessens and some Supermarkets). You need the mixture to hold together but to be rather crumbly.

Form it into balls which then can be slightly elongated. Haggis comes in several sizes. The smallest being around 1lb (half a kilo) the larger ones can be a couple of Kilos. So you don't have to be too accurate in your sizing. Just don't put too tiny a Haggis on a huge dining table!

Next take a 3:1 mix of translucent and white with the tiniest scrap of ochre to very slightly yellow it. This is for the skin. For authenticity you then need to put some thin rolls of this over the brown Fimo ...

Step 2

before adding the skin which should be rolled as thinly as possible. If you're using a pasta maker set it to the thinnest setting and then stretch it even a little more with

your fingers.

Cut a rectangle to go around and to be slightly longer than the length of your haggis and wrap it round until the edges meet in the middle.

Step 3

Trim if necessary

Step 4

Then gather the sides up like a sweet wrapper ...

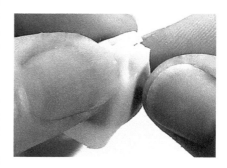

Step 5

and carefully tie cotton thread round the ends. Make sure you don't pull too tightly otherwise the thread will cut right through the clay.

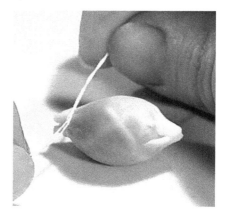

Step 6

Before you oven harden the Haggis cut through it and gently open slightly.

Margaret Rushton 'Miss Margaret's Hats'.

This Whisky bottle was lent to me by Hollytree Dolls. You can get some very

Step 7

You'll then need to use a cocktail stick or a pointed tool to drag a little of the Fimo mix back out of the 'bag'.

Why not decorate your doll's house for Burns night (makes a change from Christmas). The miniature tartan fabrics are hard to get hold of. Fortunately I knew a woman who could! These came from

nice whisky Bottles and tumblers from The Miniature Pub.

The Poinsettias were my first attempt at 'cold porcelain' flowers using Diane Harfield's new instructional video. I couldn't stop making them once I got started. Shh! Don't tell the Fimo Police! Och aye the noo!

Wheelbarrow Of Vegetables

Originally published in Dollhouse Miniatures Magazine March 2003, although many of these techniques first appeared either in my videos of 1997-99 and/or my first book Making Miniature Food

A very English scene.

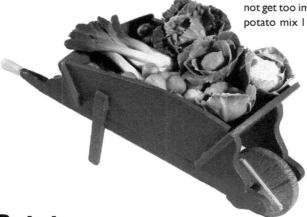

ground would be covered in earth. At my last visit to Philadelphia Miniaturia a kind lady came up and whispered in my ear that American potatoes don't have earth on them. Is this true? I'd like to know where you grow your potatoes then!

There are regional variations in the colour and quality of earth but let's not get too involved in that! The basic potato mix I use is (approximately) 50% translucent. 25% white and 25% cream coloured Fimo with just a tiny scrap of ochre, but any polymer clay will do. You need to mix a pale translucent cream colour. Roll little potato shapes. Try not to make regular little balls, they need to be elongated and

Potatoes

The potatoes are very easy to make. This is just to get your hands into the clay and doesn't take any cleverness at all! We often forget that potatoes straight from the

of different sizes. There's no grading in the garden! I then roll them all in an ovenproof bowl with a little of what I call 'scenic scatter' (that's the material model railway makers use for earth.). I oven set the clay in the bowl (including the scatter) and immediately after bringing it out of the oven I pour (drizzle) in a little matt earth colored acrylic paint. You'll need to stir it very briskly so that the material sticks to parts of each potato but not to all of it. Don't use too much paint or you'll end up with a brown blob!

Cauliflowers

The techniques for making cauliflowers, cabbages and leeks are in my books available from my website angiescarr.co.uk and there are also links there to YouTube videos of the same items too.

Step 1

Cauliflower centres use the same colour of clay so be sure to mix plenty. I would make the cauliflowers before the potatoes because you need to make a fairly large quantity of the colour. To make a cauliflower head make up a fairly large amount

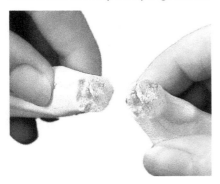

of the cream colour and form it into a roll. Holding both ends of the roll, very quickly pull it apart. This forms a rough surface. Use your finger end gently to pat back any loose pieces. Squeeze behind the surface, this forms the stalk and makes the surface 'bulge' to form the cauliflower head. Alternatively, use my cauliflower head mould available from my website.

Step 2

Add leaves to the outer edge of this stalk. You can use a toothpick or pointed tool to perfect the rough surface. You then surround the cauliflower head with fairly light coloured leaves.

The leaves are made by a 'caning' technique used by jewellery makers (also known as millefiori) I use this technique

as the mainstay of my miniature work It is what I'm known for and this is one of the simplest ways to learn it. I briefly cover it in the cabbages section next, and more thoroughly on my YouTube videos.

Cabbages

You will need leaf green clay, very light translucent green and for cauliflowers also use pale cream mix. You may like to make darker and lighter leaves by altering the basic mix once you are familiar with the method.

Step 1

Soften the leaf green and form a cylinder approx. 3/4 inch deep. Cut the cylinder in half down the centre with a single sided blade but leave the two halves close together. (This helps you to stay focused on 'which-bit-goes where'.) Make two diagonal cuts in each half right to the centre line. Roll out the very light green

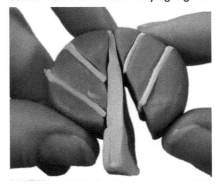

into a very thin strip and use this to put a layer in between each of the sections. Do each side separately and then add a strip between the two halves, you can make the bottom of this last strip wider for more realism.

Step 2

When you have put these pieces back together you can add extra veins by cutting out triangles on each larger vein and adding in even thinner strips of colour.

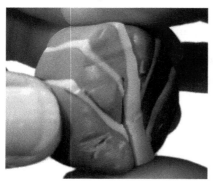

Lengthen the cylinder by squeezing in the middle of the wheel shape. You can then roll to length. Don't miss out the squeezing process otherwise the colours don't stick together and you lose definition. Stop rolling when the cylinder is approximately 1/2 inch in diameter.

Step 3

Take a small piece of Fimo (any green leftovers will do) about the size of a pea and squeeze one end to form the centre of the cabbage and stalk. Use this stalk

part to hold on to throughout the rest of the 'operation'. To make flat leaf cabbages, cut a very thin slice (leaf) off the cylinder and wrap it over the top of this little ball .

Step 4

Continue adding leaves curling the tops over a little. It is at this stage you could use slightly darker outer leaves (up to three colour changes can look very effective). Trim the stalk to a reasonable length and oven set according to the manufacturers instructions.

Step 5

For Savoy cabbages, cauliflowers and 'curly' lettuces I use my own veiners (available from my website) to add a little texture. Veiner #2 for the Savoys, or original #1 for cauliflowers, and #4 for lettuces.

Step 6
The finished savoy and cauliflower.

Leeks

You will need Leaf green clay with a little translucent added, 50/50 white/translucent mix and a spring green mix which is made from leaf green, yellow with a little white and translucent.

Step 1
Now I use a method known by polymer clay enthusiasts as The Skinner Shade technique (named after Judith Skinner, who discovered this method of producing gradually changing hues in polymer clay). Assemble triangles of colour as shown. Rather than the standard Skinner Shade method of going directly through from white to dark green which produces unrealistic hues in the middle of the leek, you change the colour to a spring green in the middle by adding a triangle of that colour. The

amount of clay you use depends on how many leeks you want to make. I recommend that you start small. When you have assembled your triangles you need to fold them in half bottom to top and roll them out (in that direction only). Fold again in the same direction and roll again.

Step 2
You'll need to do this several times but you'll soon see the blending starting to happen. A pasta machine is an excellent investment if you are thinking of making a lot of miniatures, and for this job it's a godsend. You'll end up with a fairly short and wide strip. What you need is a long and thin one.

Step 3
Persuade the strip into a narrower longer strip by gathering to the middle and then lengthening. This is a little difficult to describe without rather a lot of pictures.

There's a more advanced method for producing the green lines within the body of the leek in my 2nd book.

Step 4

Leaving a little of this strip for the centres, re-roll the rest in your pasta maker on the thinnest setting. You will have to have a large tile or working board ready

to take the strip which will need cutting into pieces approximately 1/6 inch across.

Step 5

Make a roll for the centre of the leek Cut nicks in the green top to form central

leaves. To this add four or five outer leaves from very thin slices positioning very care-fully to line up the colour changes. Keep the tops of the leaves slightly open. Pat the base of your leek on a piece of rough sandpaper to form the root area.

Draw fine lines in the leek stem and leaves with your pointed tool it is easier to draw on the leaves when they are laid on the surface on which you will harden them. You can pick the leek up and tap the bottom on some very coarse sandpaper to produce the texture of the root part.

Step 6

I make all the elements separately, harden them, and then glue them into place. However I hold my hand up to the fact that the leeks shown in the picture are moulded from an impression made of a single leek. Again, the mould is available from my website.

Pomegranates

Originally published in DHMS Magazine Issue 106 April 2003

Internet for historical references to the pomegranate, Pomegranates (pome garnad in those days) first appeared in the UK in medieval times. I imagine they could have been brought back by the crusaders. By the Middle Ages they appeared in English recipes but would only have been available to the wealthy classes. So forget putting them in a tiny Tudor house! One recipe mentions them in combination with strawberries so I rather imagine they would have been preserved in vinegar since the two arrive at different times of the year.

If brought in from the Middle East or Southern Spain (the pomegranate was the emblem of Catherine of Aragon) you would certainly be waiting until Christmas for your new stocks to arrive! Pomegranates are also used as a symbol of fertility (all those seeds I suppose) and images of the pomegranate were often used in Elizabethan blackwork and in surprisingly early wallpaper and fabric designs. These designs were re-used or re-worked by Arts And Crafts designers. Bowls of pomegranates always look exotic with other fruits and you could colour them with gold powder for 'decorative purposes' (I won't mention the 'C' word for a few more months!)

Forgive me dear 'superclayers' for explaining again for the benefit of the readers who are new to the magazine what a 'cane' is. Caning is a technique exactly like millefiore in glass or the techniques used for making seaside rock. Beginners might like to visit my website angiescarr.co.uk for a simple step-by-step tutorial showing how to make 'peelable' miniature oranges by a really simple caning technique, and there are also links there to YouTube videos of

What at first sight might seem a really difficult challenge turned out to be surprisingly easy.

Pomegranates appear towards the end of the year but I, like the fashion industry, have to think ahead of time. (How's that for an excuse?). Our editor Janet herself came up with this challenge for me.

To me Pomegranates mean Hull Fair. Along with coconuts, nougat and coconut ice, biting cold and rain. It's always the first sign of winter. I've always had a desire to make a little Hull Fair. But, you know 'little elements are us'. I never get around to the big miniature projects (pardon the expression) and only ever seem to make the 'parts'.

However here are a few ideas for using Pomegranates in your Dolls houses. As far as I can ascertain from trawling the various items. Once you understand the principle you'll be 'caning' with the best!

The principle is that you build up your clay in a short fat cylinder and then you lengthen it to reduce the scale. So you need to notice how the object you are trying to replicate is made up. Pomegranates are made up of many tiny seeds surrounded by very translucent red to pink watery sacs. These are clumped together almost randomly and enclosed in yellow, papery membranes. These are then enclosed within a tough leathery outer skin of the same yellowy colour. The outer skin is coloured with a 'blush' of pink but this is often accompanied by various hues of green and brown. In some species even purple.

Step 1

I used Red translucent Fimo from the Fimo soft range mixed 1:1 with translucent Fimo. Firstly I made a simple large-ish cylinder of yellow (white, translucent and a little yellow and ochre) surrounded by this mix. This is to make the one individual seed shape from which all the others are made.

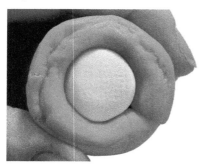

Step 2

I lengthened this cylinder into a very long 'snake', which I cut up into many inch-long pieces. I pinched each piece slightly along the edge to make it more tear shaped than cylindrical and then I assembled the pieces together looking very carefully at a real pomegranate.

Step 3

I wrapped clumps of these pieces together within a thin sheet of yellow, which I rolled out very thinly on my pasta maker. The whole thing was then wrapped in a thick sheet of yellow. The cylinder is then squeezed and then rolled to reduce the scale.

Step 4

The illustrations should show you the process of making the tiny fruits from the cylinder. You close the end off by gently 'persuading' the outer skin to cover the inside ...

Step 5

and then cut off a half pomegranate (Don't forget to cut between the two ends you have just enclosed, if you cut in the other direction you'll just get lines of colour). The flower part looks like a tiny inward pointing crown. I hollow it out with a ball tool.

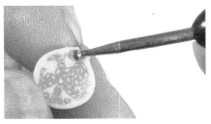

Step 6

I used sugarcraft powder colours for the delicate shading on the skin. Sue Heaser recommends using ground up pastels on Fimo and some people prefer paints. The choice is yours but any powders you use should be used before baking. Any paints, after.

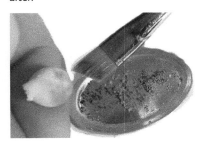

Step 7

The stalk end I made as I make apple stalks, by extruding some brown clay through a clay gun and hardening first. Then I just poke it into the soft clay. Fimo has an added advantage that you can cook it many times. This means you can make some delicate elements separately, like lobster feelers and flower stalks etc.

Step 8

I don't cut into the crown end until after it's oven hardened. Then I snip into it to form tiny points.

Step 9

You don't need to use caned material for whole pomegranates of course; you can just get away with the basic yellowish colour. I added an extra blob of material to the top to make the flower part, otherwise it can be a little difficult to get it to 'raise up' enough to make the little crown.

I used a little semi matt varnish for a slight sheen but you can just buff to a polish on a little fabric, as long as you use enough coloured powder so it doesn't all rub off.

Melons

Originally published in Dollhouse Miniatures Magazine June 2003

Watermelon, Canteloupe, Piel De Sapo!

The methods I use are very much for multiple production. However, as we say in England, there is more than one way to skin a cat (unpleasant image, I think). Melons do lend themselves to caning techniques although you can make them one at a time. I had a great email from Cindy Von Dohln-Pater who, while asking me for advice came up with a suggestion which she hadn't tried yet but which seems to me to be the best way to make a single watermelon. Cindy's method produces an arguably even more realistic result. The only problem is I had to fit the skin round very carefully and this is very time consuming.

Cindy's method (not shown)

Roll a pea sized ball of translucent red Fimo in a few poppy seeds. Add more of the same colour to the outside by wrapping it and carefully trimming to join it evenly both in the middle and by cutting triangles out of the top and bottom to fit it together. Repeat the process with the skin which you should make by stacking together pale green and dark green and rolling out into a thin strip. Make sure you join the skin very carefully to avoid seeing large streaks of the underneath colours. Then you can simply cut it open, almost anywhere you wish though using the middle to cut from rather than the 'patched' ends is usually most successful.

The nice thing about Cindy's method is that it does leave empty spaces and air gaps around the seeds which is very realistic.

Watermelon

My caning method is for mass production really. So this is for the real 'makers'.

Step 1

Take a full block of translucent red Fimo (which is in the 'soft' range) and condition the clay by mixing it very well, you'll need clean hands for this job! take off a small piece, maybe a tenth of the total, and put that to one side. Form the large piece into a short fat triangular prism shape. Cut this shape in half down the centre.

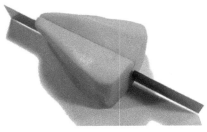

Step 2

On each half, in the same place, indent a half cylinder groove using a knitting needle or a paintbrush handle. This is so you can insert the cylinder of dark brown without distorting the shape too much. Close it back together around the dark brown.

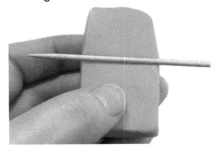

Step 3

You then need to lengthen this shape. This is where people go wrong most often! Here's a tip. Squeeze it fairly firmly in the middle, giving it a waistline! Then you know the clay is really sticking together.

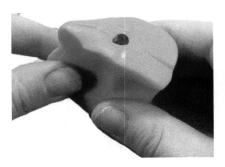

Step 4

Then you continue to squeeze along it's length towards the ends. You may find it helpful to lay it down on your working board and pull and press alternately to stretch it. At this stage the triangle is likely to thin out a bit, and actually it needs to so that you can get enough sections in

your melon. Try to keep the integrity of the triangular profile though. You'll need to stretch it until you can cut it in half and have two halves both at least a foot in length.

Then you cut it into strips of around an inch long and stack them together, on end, into a circle. Fill the centre of the circle with the saved bit of translucent red.

Step 5

Then you need to make the skin. You'll need two colours. 1) A nearly translucent greenish white, and 2) a nice dark green (leaf + a little navy). Roll both of these into a strip and add the two strips together and roll again (I use a pasta maker for this job to

get nice even strips). To get the best result, roll the whitish colour just a little thicker than the green. Wrap this skin around the main cylinder cutting and joining as neatly as you can. Lengthen this cylinder until it is around one inch in diameter then cut through the centre.

Step 6

Don't cut it into pieces but close up the end on one of the halves by gently squeezing the end and 'persuading' the outside to close over the inside. I do this by rolling the cylinder gently between the thumb and forefinger of my left hand while at the same time gently 'tweaking' at the end with the thumb and forefinger of my other hand. Then you cut this end off as if you were making just half of a watermelon. Close the other end in the same way. You can then cut into the side of the melon to reveal the seeds.

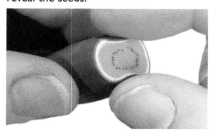

Step 7

Do not cut end to end where you have just closed it but start your cut between these two points and cut at 45 degrees to

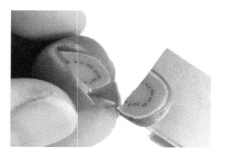

the ends. This may take a bit of practise but you'll soon get the idea!

Sharilyn

Step 8

For the pink flesh Sharilyn melon. I use a mix of translucent yellow and translucent red to get this effect about 3:1 mix. You might also like to add a little white and translucent Fimo to 'cool' the colour and

translucency a bit . The seeds are made by wrapping a teardrop shape of champagne & ochre mix with a little brown Fimo.

Step 9

This is lengthened in the same way as the watermelon sections, cut into pieces

and stacked to make one side of the centre. You'll need to lengthen this again a little and cut into two pieces. These form the two sides to the seed part. Put just a thin strip of the flesh colour in between these two halves. Then you enclose the whole with a fairly large quantity of the flesh colour. The skin is added around the outside of the cylinder and the whole thing is lengthened in the same way as the watermelon.

'Piel de sapo'

Step 10

I use a mix of translucent and white 3:1 with just a little green added to tint it. You'll need to use a cane with an oval profile so that you end up closing the ends as more of a strip down the sides to form the American football shape.

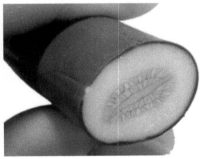

Step 11

Strange that the marks on a melon should be called 'netting' as I've always used fine net to paint that effect onto the skin. I didn't know what it was called until I did my research for this article. To make the netting effect on the outside, you simply

use a piece of fine mesh net dabbed into some light fawn or brown paint. Remove the excess that forms between the mesh as much as possible and then roll the melon against the net. You can do this either before the oven setting process or after.

Step 12

The lines are made by running the shaft of a craft tool or a cocktail stick over the surface. On the pink flesh melon I used craft powder in the lines to accentuate them.

Pick out the melon seeds by pricking

and marking with a pointed craft tool or a cocktail stick.

Display the cut pieces on a dish or marble cutting board.

Rubbish

Originally published in Dollhouse Miniatures Magazine October 2003

Angie makes Rubbish!

They say, over here, that dogs often look a bit like their owners. Or that owners choose dogs that look like themselves. Don't you find that Miniature collectors dollshouses reflect their personalities?

Some, like their owners, display an exactness in every detail. Others are more quirky. These are the dollshouses (and their collectors) which most appeal to me. One of the things which can make a scene for me is the transient 'happening'. The spilt milk, the dirty child, the trash! That's what we in Yorkshire, England call 'gritty reality'. I'm afraid this months projects reflect my home life rather too closely!

Some of the items in your 'trash' you can find in previous issues of Dollhouse Miniatures. The melon and the banana skin have both appeared. Or visit my website angiescarr.co.uk there are links there to

YouTube videos of various items including fishbones, which are also in my book Making Miniature Food. Here are a few more trashy ideas from the very simple to the complex.

Apple Core

Step 1

Apple cores are really simple. You make a sandwich of translucent/white mix with just a very thin strip of red on the top and green on the bottom. You can use red or green at both ends if you wish

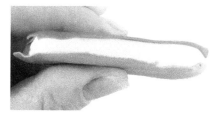

Step 2

Then you need to cut this into tiny cubes.

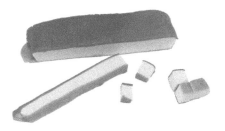

Step 3

I make apple stalks by extruding brown clay through a Kemper clay gun, oven bake them first and when the strips are hard I push the stalk firmly into the red end of the little cube. It's difficult to judge at first but it really needs to go in about half way.

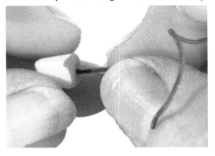

Step 4

Then you carefully 'scoop' out the sides of the cube all the way round with the end of a scalpel. The safest way to do this is

to use a very pointed scalpel and to touch the top of the cube with your finger end to hold it down. Then, be very careful to work only away from yourself towards the work surface. If you do it properly, at some point you will reveal the other end of the stalk. This makes up the pip. I forgot when making this display to touch the edges with a golden brown paint to make the core look a bit older but I highly recommend this.

I used to use Humbrol clear colour No 1322 but I believe it is discontinued. You can use ochre and brown colour pastels or powder and varnish instead.

You can make up a trash pile or a trash can with bits of just about anything you make in miniature. I make potato peelings by rolling a little ball of magnolia coloured Fimo in the dust from tea bag packets. I then simply 'peel' the top layer off and arrange it on my trash pile. I make melon skins and cheese rinds when I'm already making the whole item and put them away for later. I've also used broken miniature pottery, end pieces from my own miniature work like bacon and meats. and found mini objects which are no longer dear to my heart, though when I bought them back in the days of my first dollshouse they may have been.

Newspaper

But the newspaper makes it some-thing special. Or rather, something really 'rubbishy'. It looks like a terribly compli-cated cane. And if it were indeed made of individual letters as mine was when I first tried it, is fiendish and takes a whole day. I credit my friend Alex Blythe (a very talented miniaturist who works in both nature and fantasy) for a simpler, yet equally effective method. Still, this is a project which shouldn't be attempted by a novice polymer clay user partly because of the cost of the clay. (You could simply photo reduce a real newspaper!) This is really for the professional miniaturist as your completed cane will last you quite a long time if kept carefully.

Step 1

You will need rather a lot of Fimo for this project, a wavy blade and a 6 inch sturdy single sided blade (both of which are available at Polymer Clay Express) and a deal of patience! I used around 400g of white/translucent mix to which I added just a speck of orange and green to take the

edge off the whiteness. I put half of this aside and formed the rest into a rectangle. Don't worry about the size too much except that it should be around the depth of your wavy blade. Cut into the rectangle with the wavy blade as shown, and insert a thin sheet of black clay.

Step 2

I punctuated this black sheet with bits of white (for spaces between the words) but this isn't strictly necessary since it really isn't obvious in miniature. Put the pieces back together and cut again a little further up.

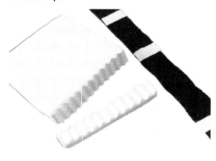

Step 3

Carry on inserting the black wavy lines…

Step 4

until the entire rectangle is filled up.

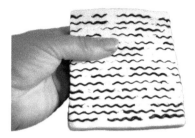

Step 5

You then need to squeeze the edges of this rectangle right in the middle alternating between squeezing the sides and the top and bottom. In this way you lengthen it until it's around 26 inches long. Cut off the end bits which inevitably distort.

You can make a photo cane by mixing up these edge bits roughly so it becomes a little grey, and making a square which you then edge with white, black and then white again.

Cut and re-stack the main cane to build up sections into a newspaper, remembering to add some of your saved white between the columns. You then add a little more white round the outside and especially at the top and bottom.

Step 6

When you have made up this cane you will need to lengthen the whole thing again.

 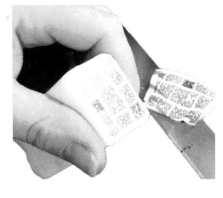

Step 7

Then it's simply a question of cutting through the middle of your cane ...

Alex Blythe's birdtable.

Never again need you worry that your miniature work is rubbish. Just make it into an art form! Here is Alex Blythe's birdtable.

Step 8

and very carefully slicing off very thin sheets. This takes a bit of practise and often works better when you leave the cane for a day to cool and 'settle'. Don't try to cool it artificially, that just causes sticky condensation which doesn't help.

Don't worry if your sheets aren't whole just thin shavings look equally effective and making them helps you practise doing sheets. Also you can use these shavings in mini pet hutches!

Coconuts

Originally published in Dollhouse Miniatures Magazine March 2004

OI! Monkey Face!

In my home town of Hull (England) we have arguably the largest travelling funfair in Europe. This takes place every autumn for just over a week and its origin dates back over seven hundred years. By tradition it was the time you could buy such exotic commodities as pomegranates, and this months how-to coconuts as well as my childhood favourites, toffee apples. Of course these days even in England you can buy coconuts everywhere at most times of the year.

The word 'coconut' is first mentioned in the 16th century. However, although coconuts were not a common sight in the everyday Victorian kitchen in England, they were common at funfairs. Mostly given away as prizes at the ever popular 'Coconut Shies' where children would throw hard wooden balls to knock the coconuts off the poles on which they were set. These poles would either be made of wrought iron, twisted into a loop at the top, or of wood, (something like an oversized golf tee). Any child would be terribly excited to win a coconut and take it home for the whole family to enjoy.

The word Coconut comes from Spanish and Portuguese word 'coco'. Explorers found a resemblance to a monkey's face in the three round indented markings or "eyes". These are revealed when the husk is completely removed.

I always suggest when making miniatures that you examine the real thing closely. You can get away with shapes that aren't quite right, but if the colour or translucency of colour is wrong you may as well not bother.

If you can get hold of a coconut, notice how the brown shell is lined with an inner shell which sticks to the coconut flesh when pulled apart. Notice how opaque and how dark this shell is. Notice the 'eyes ' when the husk is not present. See how the flesh is very white with a certain degree of translucency and how the stratification runs inward. I decided to make my coconut using a cane (a roll).

You will need 4 times as much white mix as you need brown mix because if you look carefully the edible part of the coconut is about 4 times thicker than the shell. Keep this in mind and the proportions should look just about right.

Step 1

For the shell mix 4 parts dark brown clay 1 part black. You should sandwich this between two layers of lighter brown made by mixing dark brown clay and Ochre in equal parts with a little orange and leaf

green. For the inner part use Porcelain Fimo, or substitute with 3 parts translucent 1 part white.

Form the translucent/white mix into a short fat cane and wrap with the sandwich of the other colours. Make sure the brown meets exactly with no overlaps.

Step 2

When you have lengthened the cane so that it is around one third of an inch wide ...

Step 3

close the outer skin over the inside part. This is done gently, 'persuading' rather

than forcing the edges to meet cleanly. No white should be visible. If it becomes too pointed just pat the end back.

Step 4

For a broken coconut cut off the main part of the cane now and use a ball ended tool to press into the centre to hollow it out.

Step 5

Don't forget also that it is very rarely that a coconut is cut cleanly. It is more often smashed leaving a somewhat jagged edge. I therefore cut a little out of my coconut bottom and repeated the process to form a matching top.

For a whole coconut you can just make the shape out of brown but you could use a failed cane. (Close the second end up a little more pointed.) I made my first cane slightly too dark so I used this one for making the whole coconuts. The fact that no-one will see the inside doesn't bother me at all! The whole and half coconuts are

then oven baked (according to the clay manufacturer's instructions).

Step 6

To add the husk to the coconut you can use some organic soil substitute which I bought from a miniatures fair in small bags, but which I suspect is just ground up coconut husk anyway. This is available at craft shops and at some pet shops as pet bedding. I ground this down finer using a pestle and mortar. I also used the smallest

I used a chopstick to hold the halves firmly while I painted the glue on and then sprinkled the brown powder over the glue. You need to use a fast grab tacky glue for this.

Step 7

Add the fibres to the bottom. Pinch these together at the top of the whole coconut shape and add more of the glue and powder.

of the fibres from the real coconut that I bought to examine, But again you can use some coconut fibre which has been cleaned and processed and which is available at craft shops. Firstly paint the area that you want covered in the fine ground

Featured baskets by Zara Ribaud-Thompson

husk. For the whole coconut this means the top first. For the halves you need to cover the bottom.

Dog Biscuits

Originally published in DHMS Magazine Issue 119 May 2004

be careful to apply for licences before reproducing packaging etc. for sale. Because there have been many transformations in packaging design and also the shape of the contents I opted for some of the most recent versions.

Step 1

To make packaging from the full size version I simply scanned the opened out packet in pieces.

Well I hope I get a medal for finally getting around to this one!

Here's an amusing challenge set for me by Pamela Wojciechowski, who is obviously a dog lover as she lives in a house she's charmingly called 'Muttley' he he he! Well I hope I get a medal for finally getting around to this one Pam. I did search the net to see when Shapes were first made but came up with nothing so I rang Katherine Teed at Nestle Purina who was very helpful and told me that Shapes were launched in 1929 and Bonio in 1932. Katherine checked for me but they don't have any copies of the original packaging, so if anyone knows where we can find any please let us know!

A small point about copyright here,. Although the company were very happy for us to print a mini version of the packaging for each of you to use personally for your individual dolls house, any reproduction for sale of the box or the Bonio shape (which is also registered) would be an infringement of copyright and you could be liable for prosecution. This applies to all commercial products so makers should

Step 2

I have to admit I got Frank (my husband) to do the slightly more tricky attaching-the-bits-back-together bit. We then reduced the size, first to a third of it's original size and then again to a quarter of that. Frank assured me that was 'near enough'. I sort of understand the maths but it still looked tiny to me. I'm a miniaturist who's natural sense of scale is just slightly bigger than true twelfth! The final size should be approximately 37mm across including the tabs.

Step 3

Unless you're an absolute purist I think it's easiest to stick to tiny squares, circles and heart shapes for the Shapes. The last two are available in the Kemper range and you can use box section metal available at model shops for tiny squares (and rectangles). Cut a small piece from a length and use it to cut the clay with. These aren't shown because I didn't use squares for these versions. You may need to keep a blunted cocktail stick for removing bits that get stuck in the cutter, or you could simply cut them by dividing up a larger square.

Step 4

If you look very carefully at 'shapes' there are tiny marks on the surface from the grille on which they were cooked. I used a tea strainer to make the marks. The Brown speckles in the biscuits are made by adding brown scenic scatter to the mix. Scenic scatter is available at railway modellers suppliers.

The colours for the Shapes are as follows:-

Translucent and white 75% to 25% forms the foundation of the lighter colours.

The very light coloured shapes simply has a little champagne added. About 3:1.

The more golden coloured one is the same mix but with a little ochre added and the pink one is the first same mix again but with the addition of a little orange and a little red to make a 'red brick' colour. I also made a nearly black and a chocolate brown. Chocolate brown is simply #77 Fimo with a little leaf green added.

Roll the mix thinly. For regular Fimo users who have a pasta maker for the purpose the next to thickest setting does for mine. It's about 1mm thickness. Simply cut out the shapes and put them on a plate or ceramic tile to bake (in the oven according to manufacturers instructions) I also used a cocktail stick to make a tiny indentation in the middle of some of the biscuits.

The Bonio were a little trickier to reproduce and I admit that they are a little large for scale. I made a single shape by hand. This took a lot of care and judicious shaping with my fingers and then a cocktail stick. It really is the shape that makes a Bonio. No wonder they registered it! It also has a dimple in each end and the word 'Bonio' across it , which I simulated with little marks. I cooked the 'master' and then finished it by scraping and sanding to tidy it up a bit.

Step 5

Two part silicone putty is a great material for reproducing shapes in polymer clay. It takes a few seconds to mix and only a few minutes to cure. I mixed up a little and then pressed it over my master. It doesn't stick and a few minutes later I was ready to make loads of copies. You just take out the original and press clay into the mould and bend it back a little to release.

[I now use Minitmold, available from my website angiescarr.co.uk, for most of my moulding]

Step 6

You can also make 'Markies', which are made by Pedigree, by wrapping a skin of the lightest colour round a central core of brown and lengthening it and then chopping into tiny pieces. Go on give your mini dogs a micro treat!

Encaustic Tiles

Originally published in DHMS Magazine Issue 123 September 2004

Being a self-builder tiles both fullsize and 12th scale are alwaysvery much on my mind

Very rarely a challenge comes along which is one which I hadn't even thought of. Although I'm very interested in period houses (that's the 1:1th scale sort!) and I buy more magazines on the subject than I do on their miniature equivalent. And though I have a particular interest in ceramic tiles that is the source of much derision in my family since I dragged my long suffering husband Frank across several miles of the parched fields of Andalucia in the baking midday sun in search of the factories where authentic Spanish tiles are made (rather than the tourist versions). In spite of this deep and abiding interest in tiles it never occurred to me to use my caning skills to try and recreate encaustic tiles. Hannah is recreating her own house which has an ornate floor incorporating encaustic tiles. Only after I accepted the challenge did I realise that her house was to be 24th scale! Sorry Hannah, though 24th scale is obviously possible, my patience is not that infinite!

Now anybody who knows about historical pottery, or watches 'Time Team' regularly will know that patterned encaustic tiles are actually made by a process of imprinting 'raw' clay tiles with a pattern which is then 'back filled' with clay of another colour. Derived from the Greek word en-kaustikos, meaning 'burnt in', this process creates a highly durable pattern which is not easily rubbed off during years of wear and tear. The technique was introduced to Britain from Europe by the Cistercians who used encaustic tiles to create the complex flooring designs in their abbeys in the 12th century. The Victorians revived the popularity of this style as their fashion resurrected an appetite for all things Gothic. Unfortunately many of the cheaper versions during this period were actually only printed. If you have true encaustic tiles in your Victorian house the original owners were probably rather wealthy.

The most popular colours for the patterned tiles were terracotta and biscuit and in Victorian times these were often laid within highly complex geometric patterns of other plain tiles of the same colours and also shades of blood red, brown, greys and blues.

I started making the tiles and then

realised that I needed more information. I found the name of the Jackfield Tile Museum on the internet and spoke to a lady in sales there. She was very helpful and sent me a CD of images, history of the Craven Dunnill Jackfield works and Museum and layouts for floors and walls containing encaustic and other tiles to make your mouth water. Since then I've seen the Museum on the Discovery Channel and I'm absolutely determined to visit as soon as I get the chance. Meanwhile try www.cravendunnill-jackfield.co.uk and it's related sites on the internet. Now don't go telling me you haven't got a computer. You have friends who have don't you? If not you're just going to have to organise a club coach trip. I can't think of a better day out for a miniaturists club!

Step 1

The encaustic tile 'cane' was made using a mixture of terracotta (now called Chocolate 77) and red Fimo. To make a true terracotta colour you can now use Terracotta 74 straight from the pack. I have marked a circle in it using a small glass, and lines across the centre for reference.

Step 2

The pieces were cut out using sugarcraft cutters for sugarcraft lace making (available from Cel Cakes).

Step 3

I then carefully back filled the material I'd cut away ...

Step 4

and proceeded to lengthen the cane.

Step 5

In order to get the right sizes I used araldite to attach some narrow tile strips to a large floor tile and worked my cane to

exactly the right sizes to fit between them. In this case a 6" tile in twelfth scale would be half an inch square. I decided I was going to cook this cane and slice it while still hot. My slices were rather irregular but I know you can get a cane slicing 'implement' from America. Hmm ... must get round to getting myself one of those!

Step 6

You may need to use a template to make up a floor. You could use a piece of graph paper to plan out your floor. Cut it to the size of your dolls house room/hall. Remember to plan carefully. Plan out your border if you're having one and then fill in the other tiles. think carefully if you have to cut your tiles in half to fit in. Which side would look less noticeable? I never finished this floor but this picture shows me pressing the pieces onto a base of double sided sticky tape. My plan was to upturn the whole thing onto a base of tile adhesive. But I ran out of the right colour tiles and that was that. Make sure you don't make my mistake and that you make enough for your whole project!

Step 7

Then I got into other methods of making tiles. I made the simple terracotta tiles by using The 'Skinner shade technique' to produce tiles of a nice uneven colour which lightened realistically towards the edges. I didn't bother to cook these before I cut the shape, because I liked the unevenness of a cut and pressed piece.

One great shortcut to laying simple tiles like this is the giveaway that came with the 100th edition of DHMS. What a shame for those of you who missed it as Janet tells me it's sold out. (You could use graph paper again). I laid the tiles on the paper and cooked it in-situ on a (fullsize) ceramic tile, as it had got stuck to the paper. If you do this make sure as you take the finished piece out of the oven that you put a second tile over the top while it cools, otherwise the paper will tend to curl and with it your perfect floor!

Step 8

The other project takes me back to my Hispanophilia or, to invent a new expression 'azulejophilia'. Ceramic tiles are called Azulejos in Spain because many ancient decorated tiles contained blue

pigments. Azul is Spanish for blue. This scanned picture of a real tile is a typical Moorish knotwork design worked out in polymer clay. To make a complex repeating pattern like this you need to cut down to the simplest part of the repeat .

Step 9

This is one eighth piece cut out from my scanned picture of the entire tile. It is probably just a little bit larger than life size.

Step 10

I made the one piece ...

Step 11

I lengthened it and cut it into 4. Then I lengthened it again and put the two side by side.

Step 12

You have to expect some wastage in this process because at each stage the ends distort a bit and there's absolutely no point in using a piece that simply does not match up.

I don't make houses so can't show any of these ideas in-situ but I hope this has whetted the appetites of anyone wanting to recreate tiles, either country cottage, Victorian or indeed Spanish houses. I'm off this week to put a deposit down on a 'casa sin tejado'. A house without a roof in southern Spain. You can be sure that tiles both fullsize and 12th scale will be very much on my mind over the next few

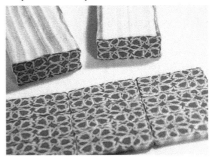

months!

[You can see how that project is going at selfbuildspain.com]

Garlic

Originally published in DHMS Magazine Issue 124 October 2004

You don't want those mini vampires to get a whiff of your blood do you?

Garlic, because it is something I've made before, I've previously dismissed as a challenge although it has been suggested a few times. But, since our editor Janet requested it recently I let it sneak in as a 'popular request' especially as I haven't made any for a long time. Infact, while working on this project I have come across a couple of shortcuts and modifications that I hadn't thought of before So everybody's happy and I have some garlic to show at Miniatura in September! Garlic should appear in every doll's house kitchen and, if you're that way inclined on every haunted house door! However it was not particularly popular between the turn of the century and the second world war after which it returned to favour. Perhaps because of our friendship with the French and possibly to flavour those insipid rations. You will need very small blossom cutters from the tiny Kemper size push cutter to the smallest blossom cutters available

from most cake decorating shops. You will need cutters of at least 5 petals. You'll need translucent, white and ochre Fimo and, if you want to make the purple bulbed garlic, a little purple powder colour. You can use craft dusting colours or ground up pastel colours (not oil pastels) or you can even raid your make up bag or better still, your daughter's make up case! (No Kira I didn't use yours!) The colour I used is Burgundy from a set of decorating chalks I bought at a craft stall at a Spanish Miniatures fair. But the chalks are an American product from a company called Craf-T. You'll also need talcum powder (talc) to keep the material from sticking too firmly to the cutter, and a needle and fawn coloured thread. To thread the whole string together you will either need raffia or you can use fawn paper covered flower wire available at sugarcraft shops. Oh and don't forget to have some scissors to hand. Embroidery scissors are best. The colour mix I've used is based on Porcelain Doll Fimo plus a little extra white (around 4:1) I like Doll Fimo for this project because it stays less sticky, even when really well conditioned, than standard Fimo. However you can make a usable alternative with translucent and white Fimo in a ratio of around 2:1. To this mix I've added just a scrap of ochre to take the starkness of the white. Be really careful how much you use. You don't want to end up with bright yellow garlic! Remember you can always add a little more of the colour but you just can't take away colour that you've already added. Everyone tells stories of adding more and more white and translucent to thin out a colour and ending up with a mountain of unusable mix.

Step 1

For the garlic strings roll out your mix to a depth of around half a centimetre thick. Cut out the flower shapes using a little talc on the cutters. You will find it impossible without talc. Use a flat backed kebab stick or even a paintbrush to push the material back out. The little indentation made by your pushing tool can be useful as it helps

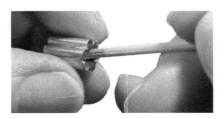

guide you when 'tucking' the ends together to form the base of the bulb, and there can still be a little gap. Anyone who has made apples and oranges and also the onions from my book will already understand this technique of 'enclosing' the ends For everyone else it's just a matter of practise and 'persuasion' but do remember that the less pressure you put on the material when handling it the better That way you don't lose the definition of the bumps which simulate the cloves of garlic.

Step 2

The other end needs nipping up and gently tweaking into a point.

Step 3

Thread your needle. Make a knot in the end of your thread by wrapping your thread round your index finger a couple of times before rolling off into what I believe is called a 'French knot' (but don't quote me on that!). This forms the root part of the garlic. Thread the needle through the centre of the garlic bulb from the base to the tip. Pull the thread until the knot becomes gently embedded into the hollow at the base of the garlic bulb so it is almost flat to the surface. At this stage you can also improve the definition of the cloves

by pressing the edge of the needle into each indentation and extending the line towards the tip of the bulb. Cut the thread off leaving at least 10 cm of thread on each bulb. You will need at least 12 bulbs of garlic for each string.

Step 4

If you want to make the pinkish colour-ed garlic at this stage you brush a really subtle dusting of colour over the rounded parts of each clove. Here again less-is-more! Put the garlic bulbs in the oven to harden at the clay manufacturer's recom-mended temperatures.

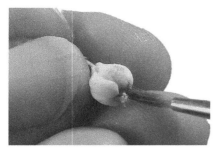

Step 5

Once they are hardened tie the bulbs together into pairs with the knot as close to the bulb as possible. Trim off the extra thread close to the knot. Make a plait from raffia or paper covered wire and add the cloves of garlic into the plaiting process starting with the three cloves and adding each pair one at a time to the plait.

Step 6

At the top tie the plait off with an extra piece of wire or raffia and trim to the desired length.

Step 7

To make the single cloves:- The simplest way to do this is simply to cut up a bulb which you have already formed! You can then colour with powder and reassemble with pieces missing.

Step 8

Extremely thin slivers of the main colour can be used to form 'papery' peeling skin. Cutting these slivers is again something which takes a great deal of practise. Be very careful when using sharp blades. You don't want those mini vampires to get a whiff of your blood do you? I can't give precise instructions on how to create these slivers because there are another type who might be after mine ... The sort who ring you up and ask you if you've had an accident recently! Now where's my garlic!

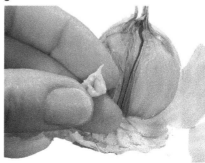

Honeycomb

Originally published in DHMS Magazine Issue 125 November 2004

This is one of the most difficult challenges I have ever had to undertake.

This month I'm accepting the challenge given me by Gerd Zacchariasson who I'd been in contact with by email and finally met last year in Copenhagen. This is one of the most difficult challenges I have ever had to undertake even though it sounds such a small thing. Or maybe because its such a small thing! To get any degree of reality it's one of those things that you really have to take a few liberties with scale. I've probably said this before, but it definitely bears repetition. Get the colour and the essence right and the scale matters less. To all of the 'anoraks' armed with 1/12th scale measures and monocles can I just say in my own defence that green is not just green. Brown is not just brown. You have to get the shade and the translucency right. Then if the shape's right too people will automatically say "Aha! That's a lettuce!" Not "well, it's a perfect sized cabbage". You go home deflated when somebody mis-recognises

something you spent hours on just because the shape and size is right but the colour leads them astray. Equally you can get the colour right and the size right but if there's no recognisable shape to your work ... well it's just a lump of plastic. ('cos that's what Fimo is, you know) But scale, you can make little adjustments (my word for mistakes) to, and it won't make a scrap of difference to most peoples response to the realism. Sometimes you have to do just that, if what makes the 'essence' of a thing is just too small to represent in a very small scale.

So here was my dilemma. Those little hexagons in honeycomb are just so small if they were made to size you would just lose them. (And hey, I'm not sure I could have found an answer to that challenge anyway. I could have tried making a honeycomb cane using my usual caning techniques. Making the scale right and perhaps exaggerating the hexagon shapes using denser colour. But the colour of honeycomb is just so subtle it would have been very hard to make them show up at all without truly unrealistic colour. And then ensuring the hexagon shapes didn't warp would be inordinately difficult. In the end I decided to concentrate on shape and colour and sacrifice scale.

The problem then is to get the right transparency for 'runny' honey. Translucent Fimo is just that. Translucent, not transparent as it is sometimes incorrectly labelled. This is merely a poor translation from the

German (Fimo is produced in Germany). So, the obvious answer is to use Liquid Fimo which is a little more transparent. Though only in small quantities. However the problem then was how to get it to be the right shape.

I sometimes push-mould Fimo in two part silicone moulds (made from Minimold available from my website angiescarr.co.uk) and have once or twice used these moulds for Liquid Fimo. I haven't been able to advise this before now because I wasn't sure that the mould would be stable at 130 degrees (centigrade) for 20 minutes which is the baking temperature and time of liquid Fimo. I have asked the manufacturer of the one I use and sell, and the chemist says that the material would not give off toxic fumes at this temperature. Because it's not manufactured for this use, all I can say is that that this is how I did it! ... There, that should cover me!

Step 1

The only thing I could think of with the correct hexagon shape was tiny allen keys. I had to scour my local pound shops for cheap packs and take out all the tiny ones. We've got a street party coming up and the second hand stall will have several packs of allen keys, all missing the smallest one! The moulding paste goes off very quickly so I didn't need to tape the keys together at all. Just held them into the base until the paste hardened (about 5 to 10 minutes).

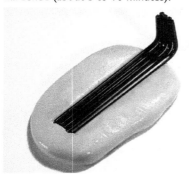

Step 2

Then I added the second layer on top. Usually if I'm making a 2 part mould I use talc to free the second half from the first.. This time I let it bond as I wanted a good tight seal so that the liquid Fimo didn't leak out. Then I pulled the Allan keys out.

Step 3

I mixed a little ochre oil paint into the Liquid Fimo to get the right colour and poured it into the resulting mould., squeezing to remove air bubbles, I wedged the mould upright with a little waste Fimo so that the liquid didn't just run out, and then I baked it.

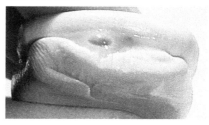

Step 4

I did have to break the mould to get the hardened 'honey' out.

Step 5

I cut this piece into slices ...

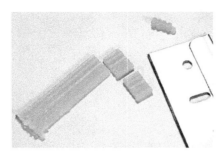

Step 6

and glued the slices together lightly using some tacky glue.

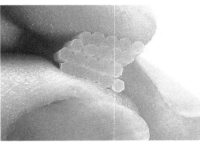

Step 7

To make the original (shown) I then rubbed a little Doll Porcelain Fimo over the top and down the sides so that it filled any gaps between the hexagons and formed a cover over the top. This did need to be very thin and subtle. Lastly I placed the 'honeycomb' into the bowl and scraped

just a little of this outer layer back at the front edge exposing the honey coloured hexagons and added a drizzle of the liquid Fimo mix before re-baking it.

Step 8

Of course it is possible to make a mould of the completed honeycomb and re-mould from that, so you don't need to go through the whole process to duplicate your work. I also decided to make jam with a mould because you can't otherwise get a raised 'blob' of liquid Fimo any other way as it is self levelling. To make raised semi liquid 'blobs' like this just make up some moulding paste and before it cures press a few times with a ball tool or the

end of a paintbrush to make an irregular indentation. When it cures it will become a perfect 'upside down' mould for jam.

The butter curls were made using a texture tool. You can use a bolt with a fairly fine thread to form the lines and just curl around a pin and push off the end before baking. So there you are Gerd, Honey ... and Jam and butter. But make mine a Danish pastry from a real Danish bakery. I know Mr Frank agrees with that!

Rocket Lollies

Originally published in DHMS Magazine
Issue 133 July 2005

Angie Scarr

I'm not used to panicking where miniatures are concerned ...

There are some events that are just 'mouthwatering' for the creative person. Some groups of people who just set each other off creatively. Some times when you just can't sleep for ideas popping into your head.

Well there's just such a group of people and just such an event every year. This year 2005 it was held in Walsall (West Midlands). Run by Hazel ... and not forgetting John, Dowd the minis4all weekend *[in those days was]* an absolute must do for anyone who wants to 'commune with the creative muse'. OK enough of all that rhetoric.

This year I've been banging on about using silicone moulds to aid the creative process. And another new favourite of mine is Liquid Fimo. The two of which you can put together to make all sorts of things that were never possible before.

For the British Miniaturists Weekend (BMW) weekend I decided I wanted to come up with a new idea that used Liquid Fimo and moulds and which couldn't be produced as easily with any other material. I also wanted to do this for the first time at BMW as an exercise in producing an idea for the first time.

By the time we arrived at Walsall I still hadn't got a new idea. I'm not used to panicking where miniatures are concerned ... well, what would be the point! So after a first evening of good company and creative ideas flowing I went to bed and slept on it. Great for creativity ... fatal for sleep. In the middle of the night I did my "oh dear I'd better get out of bed and write this down before I forget it " routine. Sometimes sleep wins the argument, and I know I've forgotten as many ideas as I've realised. But this time I knew it was important so I jumped out of bed and scribbled 'rocket lollies' on a piece of paper. Then went back to sleep.

Of course rocket lollies were going to take a little more work but I did want to unveil the basic idea of getting the three colours of 'tutti frutti' lollies moulded in Liquid Fimo. I believed multiple colour mouldings were going to work because I'd already made false teeth by this method. but I hadn't quite worked out how to make the original mould, or how to stick the lolly stick in without it showing on the surface or lying sideways in the mould.

Here's how we did it. I say 'we',

because I was helped by my gang, a group of minis4allers who helped me test out a few ideas and theories. I'm really bad at remembering names but I'd like to thank Cilla, who was definitely my right hand woman in these experiments. Together we all set about attempting to make as many lollies as possible to hand out to people at the end of the weekend.

First we made moulds using the end of a wooden stirrer, the sort you get at coffee houses. These sticks just happen to be around the right shape and size for a twelfth scale lolly. I realised when I got home that it was much easier if I went back to my local coffee house. (no flagrant advertising ... but mine begins with S and they're at The Junction in Hull) and asked them very nicely if I could take a few more stirrers than my coffee actually needed. You have to cut off the ends, a little longer than you actually need and mark the depth you want to use. You can use the rest ot the stirrer to cut into lolly sticks. This is best done (in my opinion) with a single sided blade.

Step 1

Then you can form your modelling material. The Minitmold that I use (now green coloured, available from my website angiescarr.co.uk) sets very quickly so you have to be ready to use it before you mix it. It 'goes off' within 2 minutes and is ready to demould in under 10 depending on tem-

perature. In a really cold room it takes a bit longer, but then so do I! There are other brands of two-part silicone mould mixture. These include one by Gedeo and one called Silicone Plastique. I'm not sure if these can be used in the oven at Fimo temperatures however, so it is wise to check with the manufacturer.

Draw a line on the stick at the depth you want the mould. Then quickly mix equal parts of the moulding material and make a small mound

Step 2

To form the lolly mould, the stick is pushed down into the mound of material...

Step 3

and you form the mould up around the line and flattened on the top. In 10 minutes maximum your mould is ready to use.

Step 4

I had already pre-mixed some green and orange Liquid Fimo for other jobs, and because I use rather a lot I have my pre mixes in Liquid Fimo bottles. But If you only have one bottle of Fimo you can use individual jam jars or small plastic pots to make different colour mixes. The nozzle on the bottle however does help for deep moulds as I will explain shortly. Coloured Liquid Fimo can be mixed using oil colours, or pigment powders, but not waterbased colours like acrylics.

We poured green first. We had a little trouble getting just the right amount because you can't see how full the mould is as it's

opaque. So we up-ended the Fimo bottle, squeezed the liquid to the end, pushed the nozzle deep into the mould and just gave it a little squeeze. This makes sure that there aren't any air bubbles left in the bottom of the mould.

The moulds with the first colour were then put into the oven for ten minutes. This isn't the full curing time for Liquid Fimo but we were short of time to get the three colours in. Then we took out the moulds and let them cool a little before putting the orange in. We found it easiest to squirt the orange in to full depth and then just remove some with a wooden stirrer, than to try and gauge the depth unseen. This then went in the oven a second time. The next problem was how to make the lolly stick stand up in the third colour. I thought of trying to build a jig to make them stand upright but eventually gave up and used translucent red Fimo soft, for the third colour. This provided the firmness to keep the sticks stable and also demonstrated that you can use both types

of polymer in the same model/mould. Since then I've tried just pushing the stick into the warm lolly, straight out of the oven. Sometimes it works … sometimes it just splits.

Step 5

Great fun when we finally started taking our first attempts out of the mould. Some had worked amazingly well, some were crooked, some just came apart but all in all it was a success. Christina Ludlam [now 'Cakey Bakey Art'] came up with the idea of using a cross thread screwdriver head to form a simple rocket lolly shape.

Step 6

The beauty of mould making is you can make moulds using just about anything as an original. You can model originals using a firm material, like wax for instance. You can soften this, push it into your first generation mould, demould when it's cool and therefore firmer. Then you sculpt this into a new and more accurate master. You can do this as many times as you like and each time make a new mould. This was how I made the master for my 'false teeth' and also for the ice cream.

The Titanic

Originally published in The Dolls House Magazine, April 2002

The Last Meal.

When Christiane asked me to produce the last dinner on the Titanic I was excited and a little overawed by the prospect. After all, in deference to those who both died and survived the terrible tragedy that befell the magnificent ship on the night of 14th April 1912 (ninety years ago) I should, at least be as true to life as possible. It is true that ninety years after the disaster and two or three years after the Film which my husband and I saw on valentines day (say Ahhh!) we have a more romantic view than we would have allowed ourselves in years gone by. The images that first come to mind when mentioning meals on the Titanic would be those of the extravagance of the early part of the last century. Of course there would also have been the simpler fare enjoyed by the passengers in steerage. I couldn't possibly cover all the fare that

was no doubt enjoyed greatly on that night oblivious of the speed the ship was reaching and the potential for danger that was to become a terrible reality. Imagine, if you will, the scene just a few hours before the tragedy. Imagine the opulence of the scene, the gaiety of the well dressed and excited passengers. The self congratulation of the designer, the owners and the captain as the ship sliced through the dark sea. Then imagine sitting down to a meal of some eleven courses all with their recommended wines and accompaniments.

The first place I looked for inspiration was a book lent to me by Christiane herself which I can only assume to be well researched and historically accurate. However first reading of the book threw up as many questions as it did answers. The most difficult of all was nothing to do with the food but the lighting at the table. I couldn't work out whether the table lamps were electric or not. In the colour illustrations there seemed to be several different types of lamps and lampshades, some of these were artists impressions only and some were from the identical sister ship the Britannic. I never really solved this dilemma as lamps seemed to be present at dinner that were absent at lunch. We know that the Titanic had electricity but there were no visible wires to the lamps. The shades however were of pleated fabric which leads me to believe that they were indeed electric table lamps.

As I trawled through for clues I realised that there were of course several different restaurants. In addition to the first, second and third (steerage class) it seems there was also an a-la-carte restaurant, which by all accounts was very popular with the 'upper class' passengers. There were also cafe lounge areas where one could 'take tea'. In actual fact the a la carte restaurant was probably the one preferred by the super-rich passengers, however many of the well known 'characters' of the Titanic's maiden voyage would have dined in 'first class'.

Only two menus survived the disaster. Since one of these was from the first class dining saloon, I finally decided to follow this menu, choosing between courses just as a diner would have done. I also decided on a table setting which would be as near as I could get to the original though I did keep down the table size to four places. On the ship many tables in the first class dining saloon were for eight although there were tables for two and four. The tables were square so the layout is similar. I cheated by using a very small cake board on a smaller table. The lampshades in the first class dining room appear to have been red pleated, however I had already bodged this pink one which is similar to the one used in the a-la-carte restaurant. (Since miniature needlecraft is not my strongest suit, I hope to get away with this.) The chairs were ample sized oak carvers with

Here is the actual menu with our choices in bold.

Menu

Hors d'oeuvre Varies
Oysters
Consomme Olga
Cream of Barley
Salmon, Mousseline sauce, Cucumber
Filet Mignon Lili
Sauté of chicken Lyonnaise
Vegetable marrow Farcie
Lamb, Mint sauce
Roast Duckling, Apple sauce
Sirloin of Beef, Chateau potatoes
Green peas, Creamed Carrots
Boiled rice
Parmentier and Boiled New Potatoes
Punch Romaine
Roast Squab and Cress
Cold Asparagus Vinaigrette
Pate De foie Gras
Celery
(The modern interpretation in the Book Last Dinner on the Titanic has these as separate courses although the menu has them placed close together as if they were 'a choice of'. Just in case..... I did them all!)
Waldorf Pudding
Peaches in Chartreuse Jelly
Chocolate Painted Eclairs
French Ice cream
The book also adds an eleventh course of
Fresh Fruits and Cheeses.
So who am I to argue.

olive green covers.

Luckily the 'table' was the right size to use a ladies handkerchief as a tablecloth. A gent's handkerchief would be suitable for an eight person setting. I folded and pressed the cloths to form nice sharp edges. One illustration in the book appears to show a fold like the one I used. I have to thank my local shop 'Hollytree Dolls' for lending me the items I needed for my table setting. Incidentally all the glassware except for the wine glasses are by Phil Grenyer. I used two sets of knives and forks plus a spoon for the cutlery, as all I could find was one style of knife in my budget. (I'm one of the have-nots who re-create rather than living it!) The table would have been laid with fish knives and forks and a soup spoon as well. I couldn't find any authentic looking champagne glasses so I laid out two sets of the 'flute' style. I know red wine wouldn't have been served with oysters but this set was already full!

There would have been napkins on the table and the White Star line had its own silver napkin rings. The menu was unlikely to be on the table it would be much more likely to be on the tables in the more informal reception room. As you can see I left these out of my table setting as well and got straight into the first course.

1 Oysters

Apparently the Titanic carried 1221 quarts of oysters when it left Southampton.

The little leaf is one of two types which appear in a few of the meals was made using a paper punch and a very thin sheet of Fimo which I rolled out in my pasta maker. The insides of the oysters were given the pearlised finish with sugarcraft pearl powder which is available at cake shops and through Holly Products.

2 Cream of Barley

This is simply a little cream coloured bathroom sealant. The squeezy bottle type which comes in a silver tube works best. This is available at DIY shops.

3 Salmon, Mousseline sauce, Cucumber

Pale pink mixed Fimo. Basically translucent with a scrap each of white, red and orange. The serving dish is a jewellery/eggcraft finding from Tee Pee crafts. The sauce ... more sealant.

4 Filet Mignon Lili

It's not too clear what this consists of but this is supposed to be a small fillet

steak with a piece of pate and a thin slice of black truffle on the top. Probably it would be surrounded like this with a wine sauce.

5 Sirloin of Beef, Green Peas, Creamed Carrots, Parmentier New Potatoes

Peas … A pain to make but there really is no other way. That is unless you cheat and use those tiny beads that Tee pee supply. But you'd have to paint them an appropriate shade of green as theirs is too bright and too translucent. For fiddly Fimo peas you need lots of translucent and only a little green and yellow., and the patience

of a saint. For best effect make two or three slightly different shades.

6 Punch Romaine

Yep, I cheated. But my friends at Holly-tree supplied these ready made. Well don't you think ten courses was enough!!!!!! If you're still unsure use scenic water coloured with a little food colouring.

7 Roast Squab and Cress

These were really fun. They were my second attempt and are the same as my chickens/turkeys but a quarter of the size.

8 Cold Asparagus Vinaigrette

There were 800 Bundles in the ships stores.

The asparagus was a delight to make and I went on to make a whole tray full over two days (so that's why the article is late Christiane!) They are made using the Skinner shade technique and

then the top bits are cut from a strip of extremely thin clay which is two different colours rolled together (purple and green) This is so complicated it would take several pages to describe. The oval plate is made of Fimo pressed and cooked on to a metal stamped plate and then removed. The gold edges are added by running a cocktail stick (which has been dipped into gold acrylic hobby paint) around the edge at a very slight angle from the upright.

9 Pate De Foie Gras, Celery

More shading for the celery and more stamped leaves. this time the colour mix is a very pale yellowish green. Of course with lots of translucent again.

10 Peaches in Chartreuse Jelly

The jelly, which I'm not really happy with was made from coloured clear casting resin. Unfortunately I added a little yellow pigment and it made it cloudy.

11 Fresh Fruits and Cheeses

Even though citrus fruits were still something of a rarity there were 180 boxes of oranges in the stores on departure. The fruit and cheeses are an addition to the actual menu from that night. The book I'm using for reference assures us that this was the normal ending for a meal. Before, that is, the retirement of the gentlemen to enjoy their port and cigars.

Plums And Asparagus

EXTRA ARTICLE Originally published in DHMS Magazine June 2012

Each year, at the end of May /beginning of June it's time for the Rheda-Weiden-bruck miniatures fair in Germany. This used to be held in the pretty little town of Soest. I mourn it's change of venue mostly because I can't get my tonsils round 'Rheda Weidenbruck'!

This area of Germany is called West-phalia and is most famous for its cured ham, and for the strange black bread called 'Pumpernickel'. However, lesser known in the rest of Europe are its asparagus and its plums. The plums known as Stromb-erger Pflaumen come from a little town very close to the miniatures fair known as Stromberger. I have it in my diary to make a visit this year. Unfortunately the beginning of June is too early for the fresh plums but I might be able to taste some of the liquors and preserves that are also made from them. However at the time of the fair the roadsides are littered with little cabins selling the fat white Asparagus. it can be really huge compared with the skinny green aspar-agus that we are used to in the UK.

Strangely they also eat a lot of it in Spain where I live now, but I've never seen it sold fresh, only in jars and tins and I wondered if it was imported from Westphalia. Looking at the jar in the cupboard and those on the shelves at the local supermarket sadly it seems they come all the way from China!

The bottled and tinned stuff to me is slightly acidic (must be the preservatives) tasteless stuff. But the fresh asparagus is really well worth buying and stuffing in the suitcase to take the short flight home.

White Asparagus

Making the white Asparagus is very similar to the green. If anything it's a little easier because the colours are all variations of greenish, yellowish white. The growers blanch them to be as white as possible. That is to say they grow them in the dark and earth them up so they form as little chlorophyll as possible.

First make a 'Skinner shade' from white to yellowish white. I use porcelain colour Puppenfimo for a semi translucent white.

Remember when buying it to ask for the porcelain colour.

Puppenfimo is only made in large blocks, so, if you don't have it you can use what I call foundation mix 2 which is three quarters translucent to one quarter white. For the other end of the 'Skinner shade' add a little yellow. I use leftovers from my lemon canes. This means that there's actually only a touch of each of the yellows That is to say, a touch each of the golden yellow and the normal (slightly greenish) yellow. If you add too much you have a terrible job trying to re-mix, so add a tiny scrap only and then more if needed. If you add too much people will have no clue what it is you've made!

If you've never made a 'Skinner shade' before it's described in my book Miniature Food Masterclass, otherwise there are several illustrations of how to make it on the internet. Green asparagus appears in the same book.

White Asparagus can be around 25cm long so you can use 2cm as a guide length for 12th scale.. Your block needs to be a little less deep to account for the length-

ening during rolling the tiny spears.

Cut slices from your basic pile and little strips from those slices.

Roll the strips between your fingers, patting off the bottom so that it's pointed at one end and flat at the other.

I need to exaggerate the tips a little for definition, I make the tips and tiny leaf

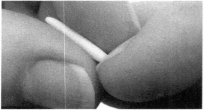

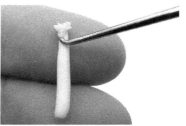

buds just a little more green. That is to say I take the yellowy mix and just 'tinge' it with green. But this mustn't be a bright green,

Next I add the almost invisible triangular buds. This seems like a lot of trouble to

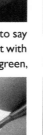

but rather a very muddy muted yellowish green added to the basic mix. Even in exaggeration ... subtlety is the key!

I form the tips by using a bent dental tool to pick tiny bits up by pressing it into the edge of the clay a few times. Then I apply the clay to the tip of the spear.

go to since they are so difficult to see even on the real thing. But if you don't do it. It isn't obviously an asparagus spear.

When making piles of asparagus, Don't bother with these leaf buds on the underneath ones as they won't be seen.

Plums

Please note, the methods I use are most suitable for larger quantities. Here I am making a fairly large cane. Beginners can start with smaller quantities and still achieve the same final effect.

When making plums and other soft fruit like peaches and nectarines, The most important considerations are the shape and relative size of the stone, and the translucency of the flesh versus the opacity of the stone and skin.

Always remember when making a cane with a central feature such as a single

central stone that that element is likely to end up bigger than you intended because the outer parts of the cane are usually warmer and therefore move a little faster than the inside when lengthening the cane. And also, when you are closing the cane to make the half plums you are using more of the outer colour to enclose the back. Leaving a little less surrounding the stone shape. You need to balance this effect by making the stone relatively a little smaller (in the cane) than you want it to appear in the final fruit.

I use Fimo effects translucent yellow (104) plus a little Porcelain colour Puppenfimo in the proportions 2:1. The Puppenfimo is just to take the edge off the translucency. I wanted it to be nearly translucent ... but not quite.

For the stone I used Fimo Ochre and then added a three dimensional look by using a Skinner-shade from a 1:1 mix of terracotta and chocolate colours.

I then surrounded the stone cane with a very thin accentuating line of terracotta mixed with a little black. (Remember, a thin line is actually a thin sheet in a 3 dimensional cane!)

If all this seems a little bit much for you for one tiny fruit stone, just use ochre bordered with a brown mix. The perfectionist in me sometimes makes me over-analyse!.

Surround the stone shape with the yellow mix. Here I've left a tiny indenta-

lapping. This is very important as overlaps will appear as big ugly blobs of clay on the tiny plum half!

Using a little translucent clay, cut a smooth curve from a piece of translucent clay, and put a curved piece on either side of a stalk piece. The smoother you get this curve, tapering out to nothing, the better shape your fruit will be.

The translucent is there because you can't have air gaps in polymer clay caning or the clay will just fill in the space and distort the shape. When you cut the cane you will barely see the translucent part.

N.B. (newbies) the next part is the most important part of caning. It makes sure all your pieces 'stick' together and extend as one rather than distorting.

Grab your cane firmly with your fingers in the middle of the 'wheel' and squeeze with a firm and even pressure. Keep moving the cane so you're press-

tion at the top and bottom. Actually the indentation at the bottom is not needed because it does depend where you cut the plum whether it's even visible or not. So if you put it in make sure it's very slight. The same with the top. I've exaggerated the indent here. I was half asleep and thinking of apples I think! In fact it's much more slight on plums and the top can be more marked on peaches and nectarines.

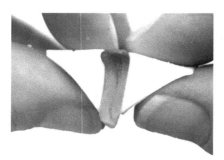

Make a purple plum skin. These plums have a very deep purple skin but there are other varieties which have different colours of both skin and flesh. I've made a two tone skin by making a sheet that is dark purple on one side and burgundy underneath. Again this is just my over-attention to detail and you can simplify just by using one purple sheet. The dark purple uses burgundy clay with a little navy blue and a little black added.

Cover the cane in the skin making sure there are no air bubbles and that the skin meets neatly at the join rather than over-

ing on different parts until you achieve a capstain shape ... Put another way ... give it a waistline! Don't be afraid of putting more pressure in the middle than the ends. What this does is 'glue' the bits together and additionally helps to expel any air that has got between the sections.

Work your way outwards towards the ends of the cane squeezing carefully until the rest of the cane is the same width as the middle. It may seem more intuitive to start rolling here but this may cause distortion or even total collapse of the cane.

When you wish to make the plums, roll a piece of cane down to just a bit bigger than the desired final size of the plum. Starting with a clean end, pinch the colour over the end of the plum to cover the yellow inside. Then just cut your plum half. I use my dental tool just to accentuate the stone bt 'drawing' round it.

so, take it easy and patiently and only roll when you have got to a stage where you want to store parts of your cane. That is to say, it doesn't need to be the final scale (e.g. 12th) but something larger that you can lengthen a little more when you're ready to use it. When saving canes for later you can wrap in cling film or plastic bags (just to keep them clean) and store in plastic tubs or old video cases. Please avoid brittle plastics as polymer clays can dissolve them.

If you're a beginner caner, you will find you have a lot of cane at the ends where the centre of the plum is not perfect. These you can use to make the whole plums. Otherwise you can make a special cane that doesn't have the stone in. I still recommend using a translucent clay in the middle and a thin skin to get the same effect.

Plums have that lovely indentation reminiscent of baby's bottoms! You can put this in using a cocktail stick, or better still a smooth pointed tool like a dental tool or large sewing needle. Just rolling it down the side to produce the line.

The plum stalks are extruded pre hardened clay. I used a clay gun to make these.

To finish the plums find a really fine smooth talcum powder and dust the whole plum before baking. After baking you can, if you want, selectively rub off a little of the white powder 'bloom'.

Of course Westphalia is also well known for it's dry cure hams. But once again I'm leaving making hams for another time.

Red (& white) onion canes

EXTRA ARTICLE Originally published in DHMS Magazine April 2012

Skill level; Advanced to Professional.

I have had many requests for the onion canes project. This project was supposed to appear in one of my books but got

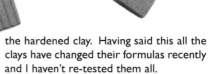

forgotten in the final draft. So here it is!

One of the most difficult canes to make, the onion cane requires loads of patience, loads of talcum powder, a delicate touch and not a little luck! The talc helps keep the layers apart and lengthening thins the material into very skinny layers just like a real onion. This cane is built up on a knitting needle to allow the rings of the onion not only to be apparent but also to fall apart, as real onion rings do, with very little effort.

You will need:-

Pasta machine or glass/acrylic rolling pin.

Short, narrow, grey coated metal knitting needle (double pointed).

Talcum powder.

Translucent clay, Burgundy clay (and Dark purple colour mix if you are making stripes).

For this project I usually use Du-kit, a New Zealand brand of clay, because of the quality and the strength and flexibility of the hardened clay. Having said this all the clays have changed their formulas recently and I haven't re-tested them all.

Great care should be taken to get the talcum powder only where it's needed and never on the joins in the clay. The technique relies on the use of talcum powder to keep the layers from sticking together. I can tell you how its done but there's a little magic in it too. Sometimes it works. Sometimes it doesn't. Good luck!

You can use translucent clay straight out of the pack for this project. If you want you can add a touch of white but if you do you must make sure you mix the clay thoroughly so there are no streaks.

Do not condition Du-kit if using a pasta machine. Du-kit has the unfortunate property of shredding in the machine on the thinner settings, but if you can learn to handle it, it has the flexibility needed to make a non-crumbling tough but flexible cane. Use it straight from the block. Cut slices off it and pass through a cool pasta maker once or twice on a thick setting. When you need thinner layers for example for the skin, pass through first on a thick setting then on progressively thinner settings.

If you can't get hold of Du-kit you can use any of the other clays in Translucent.

Step 1

First of all prepare a large quantity of your translucent material in thick sheets. Your results will be more even with a pasta machine set to the thickest setting. Then make the thinnest possible sheet of the burgundy mix. Put the two together and re-roll on the thick setting to remove any air. Or just press the thin sheet onto the thick translucent and smooth down by hand or with your rolling pin. But do make sure all air is removed. You'll need a narrow piece just wide enough to go right round the knitting needle, and several pieces of increasing width for the different layers.

You are likely to use a large amount of clay, at least one whole large block if using Du-kit. To minimise the quantity use a shorter needle or cut one down. But you will need a minimum 4 inches/ 10 cm of needle to make it easy to handle.

For extra realism you can make the burgundy layer striped using my onion skin technique described in my first book.

Step 2

Start with the narrowest knitting needle you can find. Powder the knitting needle with talcum powder and wrap the needle. With a layer of clay. Translucent side in towards the needle

You may need to put a slight angle on the clay to make it meet neatly. It is VERY important that you don't get any talcum powder on the edge of the strip after cutting it, so that the join sticks together well.

Step 3

If you don't want your onions to fall into rings you can just stick the next sheet straight on to the first. If you do want rings, talc this first layer well, avoiding the ends (just beyond the ends of the needle) as you will need to stick the next layer on to the first.

Step 4

Add talc to the white side of the next layer. Do this before you cut the edges which join together. Cut the edges of the final join when you're sure it's the right size. Press the two edges together with your thumbs forming a little ridge (but not an overlap) to make sure it's fully bonded. Take your time with this, and then smooth the join down flat. If it comes apart, re-cut and try again. It's really not worth carrying on unless it's fully bonded.

Again, don't forget leave the very ends talc free so that you can pinch them together to stick them to the first layer. If you don't do this your cane will not lengthen successfully.

sure your hands are clean so that the clay neither sticks to your hands too much, nor slips around too much.

Do this lengthening process while it is still on the needle as much as you can. The ends will start to lengthen off the needles and you will end up with a nice, straight, but quite unwieldy length of clay at best! At worst it will all go wrong at this stage. I did warn you it wasn't easy!

Step 6

When you feel it is all lengthening well and is nearly down to scale (that is to say smaller than 1/6th scale) cut in half down the centre of the needle

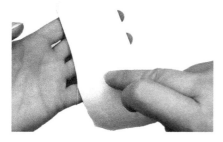

Step 5

Repeat another 2 or 3 times until you have a fat little sausage with pinched up ends.

Start to lengthen the cane by hand, by a combination of rolling and squeezing between your fingers, (or even squeezing in your whole palm), and pulling. Do not roll it on the table at this stage. This is tricky, and the looser canes will try to bag and bulge and even separate and tear. All I can say is try to stay in control! Make

Step 7

and slide each half carefully off the needle, keeping in control of the cut end so that you can pinch the separate layers together and continue lengthening from the end furthest away from this cut, working towards it until you are happy that the scale is as you want it. For onion rings you can bake at this stage and slice afterwards. Remember, the ends will be wasted.

These rings can be used for salads, stews, pizzas etc. and as seen on the preparation boards at the start of the article.

Step 8

If you want to make whole onions as well as rings join together the bottom end by pinching together until they stick, Put a tiny ball of translucent clay in the end to help it stick together and make it look more realistic.

Step 9

The top end is pinched to a tip. It takes a little practise to 'gather' the inner layers together for this. Actually it's easier to make the tip end first when you're practised.

Step 10

Then you can cut in half top to bottom, or across the middle either before or after baking.

Professional tips:

Tightly fitting lightly powdered layers will make the cane lengthen easily. A looser fit and more powder will make the onion rings separate more easily. But the cane will be really difficult to handle and lengthen, so this should only be tried by experts.

If you'd like a striped skin as in step 1 you should make a stack of burgundy and navy, then slice and join this and roll out before attaching to the white layer. This technique for making a striped skin is described in my first book Making Miniature Food.

Step 11

You can also do the same project with white onions using a translucent and green stack to make the skin.

Step 12

When I make white onion rings I only put the green stripes on the outer layer they aren't seen throughout an onion anyway.

Troubleshooting:

The most common problems that occur when making onion canes are

- *Getting talc on the joins which causes separation and incomplete rings.*

- *Getting talc on the very ends which causes the several layers to lengthen at different canes causing a 'baggy' cane which won't lengthen properly.*

- *Not using enough talc between the layers which causes the layers not to separate when you want the rings to part after cutting.*

- *Having sticky hands which can cause the very thin layers of clay to stick to your hands and shred when lengthening.*

- *Not baking at a high enough temperature which causes the rings to shatter when you try to slice them.*

If buying Du-kit for this project get a large block of translucent, two small blocks of burgundy and a small block of navy blue to make a red onion cane.

Acknowledgements

Among many others:-

Gail and Aileen Tucker for historical facts

Barbara Leuchtenberger

Christiane Berridge

Alex Curtis (now Blythe)

Sue Heaser

and for constant support over the years:-

Nicola Croad

Hazel and John Dowd

And my lovely and supportive husband, (boss ... and slave) Frank Fisher who edits all my pictures and text, and is the protagonist behind all my published work including this collection.

Apologies to the hundreds of friends and customers who's names I couldn't fit here but who's support is consistent and always very much appreciated.

Contact details for magazines featured

Dolls House and Miniature Scene Magazine

www.dollshousemag.co.uk

Dolls House Projects

www.dollshouseprojects.co.uk

Dollhouse Miniatures Magazine (USA)

www.dhminiatures.com/

The Dolls House Magazine

www.thegmcgroup.com/

Index

CPSIA information can be obtained
at www.ICGtesting.com
Printed in the USA
LVHW012225070121
675967LV00010B/815